The Warrior Life:

What it is and how to live it.

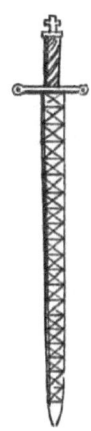

Presenting the Five Warrior Attributes

by

James T. Slattery

First printed by CreateSpace 10/31/15

ISBN-13: 978-1512196764

ISBN-10: 1512196762

Cover Art: Crusader Knight's shield.

9th century sword in sheath with a cross-shaped pommel. From the illustrations in the bible of Charles II. Le Chauve (840-887).

Scripture quotations are from the International Standard Version Bible® Copyright © 1996-2010, http:// http://isv.org.

Used eSword® Bible Software, Copyright © 2000-2014, for scripture research. Please support their ministry at http://www.e-sword.net/support.html.

Printed in the United States of America

Also by James T. Slattery

The Warrior Life Field Manual

Camp Life in the Northern Kingdom:

Memories of Frosty Mornings and Cold Nights
in the Company of Men

and

An Adirondack Sanctuary

In My Time

The Adam Commission Report

Menaissance: The Literary Journal of Men

All available on amazon.com

Dedication

This book is dedicated to the memory of a Warrior.

PFC DONALD J. SLATTERY, 32377286
Third Infantry Division
15th Infantry Regiment
F Company Medical Detachment
World War II
Born: 10 January 1920
KIA: 1 March 1944, Anzio Beachhead

Italy, 1943
Donald J. Slattery is on the far right.

Contents

Preface

Exodus 15
³The Lord is a warrior;
Yahweh is his name!

It's really very simple – God is a Warrior.

Unfortunately, this Truth is either denied or distorted through the teachings and missions of almost all Christian denominations who have for centuries self-servingly portrayed God as passive, benign, soft, effeminate, maternal, and companion animal friendly who suffers a lot and very deeply with a somewhat manic-depressive personality who endures life with demure passive high-minded acceptance of his woeful Fate.

Where is the One who commanded villages to be wiped-off the face of the earth? Who depopulated entire geographic regions, (including livestock, cats, dogs, and anything else that breathed around them) because they weren't living according to His commandments? Where is the One who threw moneychangers out of the temple overturning their tables and whipping and kicking them to the gutter where they belonged? Where is the One who admonished Mosses by saying, "Why are you crying out to me? Tell the people to get moving". (Exodus 14:15) In other words quit your whining and get it done!

Hebrews 13

⁸Jesus Christ is the same yesterday and today and forever.

Our Warrior God hasn't changed however how He's perceived has changed over time to everyone's detriment. Our modern God is less Warrior-like making Him more acceptable to Woman, Children, Sinners, and "Churchmen" who are infinitely more comfortable with a benign feminine socially aware politically correct really-nice God who doesn't hold a grudge and makes you feel better because He's so forgiving of your many foibles. The Truth is God is a Warrior and He's perfect. He's the Alpha and Omega. He's omnipotent and omnipresent and the most powerful being that has ever or will ever exist.

Revelation 1
[8]I'm the Alpha and the Omega," says the Lord God, "who is, and who was, and who is to come, the Almighty."

Mark Edmundson writes about God's True nature in his book entitled Why Football Matters pages 106-107.

To put it crudely: There's nothing pacifist about the Yahweh of the Hebrew Bible. He has nothing to say about turning the other cheek or about forgiving anyone seven times seven. Yahweh drowns nearly the whole world when he gets exasperated at its sinful ways; he destroys Sodom and Gomorrah in a blink; He murders the firstborn of the Egyptians; he drowns Pharaoh's army under the rolling Red Sea.
Yahweh is also the creator God, of course. Out of his love He makes the heavens and the earth, the seas and the stars. He gave life to Adam by taking up a handful of clay and breathing into it. His connection with His creatures, especially those He favors, is strong and deeply loving. He is a generous and watchful Father to his people.
But He can also be a wrathful figure who makes violent demands. When King Saul conquers the Amalekites, the Lord tells him that he must kill every living being: man, woman, child all the way down to the livestock. Saul spares a handful of them, no more. The Lord becomes so enraged with him that He decrees Saul's kingship must come to an end. The prophet Samuel nearly kills Saul in God's name. As the Bible unfolds, Yahweh seems to become less vengeful and more humane. The

prophets Isaiah and Jeremiah beseech Him to care for the poor and the widows, and sometimes He no doubt listens.

Distorting God's Nature shrouds us from His essence and teachings increasing our separation from Him making our earthly lives less Joyful and our afterlives less certain. By softening Him we decrease significantly the power of His Truth that He reveals to us in the Bible. For example God commanded the Israelites to "take possession of the land". Being a Warrior He commanded them to "take" it.

Deuteronomy 10
[11]So the LORD told me, 'Get up and proceed to lead the people, so they may enter and take possession of the land that I promised to give their ancestors by an oath.'"

Although God could have simply given the land to the Israelites He didn't because He knew they had to sacrifice something for the land and The Covenant to warrant and appreciate their blessings. There's no free lunch. God calls Men to sacrifice their lives by being Warriors so they and theirs will receive the blessing of the The New Covenant. The good news is that He is always with us supporting and guiding us in our Walk. God has revealed to us the Attributes and behaviors of Warriors.

1 Chronicles 12
[1]The following Men joined Dave at Ziklag while he was hiding from Saul son of Kish. They were among the warriors who fought beside David in Battle. All of them were expert archers, and they could shoot arrows or sling stones with their left hand as well as their right. They were all relatives of Saul from the tribe of Benjamin. Their leader was Ahiezser son of Shemaah from Gibeath; his brother Joash was second-in-command.

...

[8]Some brave and experienced warriors from the tribe of Gad also defected to David while he was at the stronghold in the wilderness. They were experts with both shield and spear, as fierce as lions and as swift as deer on the mountains.

In summary a Warrior:

1.   surrounds himself with Warriors.
2.   masters personal protection, weapons, and is physically fit.
3.   is mentally tough and perseveres.
4.   is wise.
5.   serves God above all else.

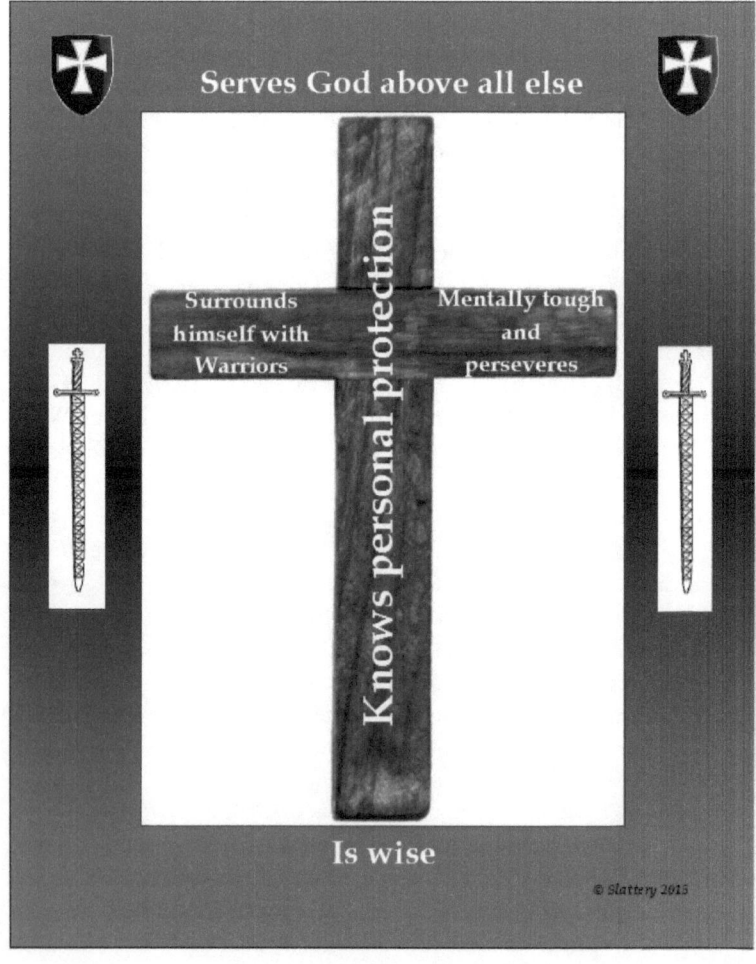

We know God's a Warrior and that He wants Men to be one also. Men have no choice. We have to be Warriors if we are sincere in wanting to live an authentically Christian life. So if we know this why is there so much resistance and distortion of the Truth? Why are we compelled to create and perpetuate myths about Him neutralizing the power He gives us to live a Joyful life while defeating Evil? Why is this Truth denied making it impossible for Men and Women to live authentic Christian lives?

People who deny the Truth that God is a Warrior are surrendering their lives to an enemy that's already been destroyed. Although the cosmic war between Good and Evil is won its battles are still being fought today and will continue to be fought long after we're gone. It's a Man's Nature and responsibility to fight in The War, be the best Warrior he can be, and to prepare younger Warriors to continue the fight.

Matthew 10

> [34]"Do not think that I came to bring peace on earth. I did not come to bring peace but a sword!

One of many battles a Warrior must fight involves Satan undermining the power of Men in society. Destroying or disabling Warriors is Satan's most powerful strategies to win The War that he by Nature must continue to fight.

Whereas the 2nd Amendment to the United States Constitution, which codifies the right to bare arms, is the most important Amendment of our Constitution because it guarantees all others so are Warriors the most important force in The War between Good and Evil because we guarantee all others.

1 Peter 5

> [8]Stay alert! Watch out for your great enemy, the devil. He prowls around like a roaring lion, looking for someone to devour.

I'm not an expert or highly proficient in all of the Warrior Attributes. However I do have a wide variety of knowledge and experience that qualifies me to write this book. In summary, I'm a National Rifle Association (NRA) Certified Pistol Instructor and Range Safety Officer, I've trained above the third level in Krav Maga, I graduated from the U.S. Army's Enlisted Basic Training, Reserve Officer Training Corps (ROTC) Basic and Advanced Courses, Army Medical Department Officer Basic and Advanced Courses, and a plethora of additional training and experiences. I earned the U. S. Army's Expert Field Medical Badge and many other achievements and accolades giving me at least a basic understanding of each of the Warrior attributes.

However, as true Warriors know the only person you should listen to exclusively and without reservation is God. With that in mind you should be very selective and discerning in the sources you use to learn about and improve your Warrior Attributes. You should qualify the source of information based on its adherence to the Truth as reveled in the bible and customize it to your unique situation.

A classic example is the debate concerning Warrior Attribute No. 2 -- Masters personal protection, weapons... -- manifesting itself in the debate over the type of firearm someone should purchase for personal protection. Holy wars have raged in the personal protection community dating back to the first wooden tubes filled with rocks and a gunpowder type substance fired with a torch. I'm sure there was a heated debate over how big the tube and rocks should be; how much gunpowder like substance one should use; the best way to hold the tube, ad nauseam.

Warriors know the best firearm to buy depends upon the unique physical, mental, and environmental characteristics of the person that's going to actually shoot it. A Warrior knows this because he studies the subject in question and has achieved at least some basic knowledge and practical experience with firearms. If a Warrior isn't familiar with the subject or experienced he knows someone who is and will use them to improve his shortcoming.

My father used to say, "It's not the big-mouth at the bar you have to worry about it's the quiet guy sitting in the corner."

Unfortunately, the mass media and the Oprahs of the world focus on the bigmouths and their behavior rather than the Warriors quietly fighting The War. They present all Men as "Frat

Boys" requiring strict monitoring and control through numerous discriminatory laws and agencies or many really bad things will happen. Yet when a susceptible population of males are controlled to their liking they become disenchanted with the situation asking, "Where are all the real Men?" As a matter of record Oprah had an entire show dedicated to Woman decrying the fact that there weren't any "Real Men" anymore.

Warriors fight daily to be the Warrior that God commands us to be while not unduly upsetting Women, Children, and Church Men. It's an impossible task creating a **Cognitive Dissonance** (Dissonance) in Men's' minds resulting from them being pressured to think and behave contrary to what their bible, hearts, and minds tells them.

> *Cognitive dissonance* is the mental stress of discomfort experienced by an individual who holds two or more contrasting beliefs, ideas, or values at the same time, or is confronted by new information that conflicts with existing beliefs, ideas or values.
>
> Wikipedia

There's an ancient story about a monk who's standing at the edge of a cliff looking out over a beautiful valley. He hears a rustling noise behind him. He turns around to see a huge Tiger stalking him from a clump of bushes. He sees the Tiger is famished and he's its prey. The monk looks over the edge of the cliff seeing a single branch sticking out. He climbs over the edge of the cliff and hangs by the branch. He thinks he can hang there until the Tiger leaves. He looks-up at the edge of the cliff and sees the Tiger resting on his paws and peering down at him. The Tiger isn't moving. The monk looks down thinking he can jump-down and run-away. He sees another famished Tiger looking up at him waiting for him to fall. The monk is stuck between two horrible alternatives. The monk looks over and sees a little bush clinging to the side of the cliff. Growing out of it is the most beautiful strawberry he's ever seen. He reaches over and picks the strawberry. He bites into the strawberry. It tastes better than anything he's ever eaten. He takes his time eating the strawberry living in the moment and forgetting his dire circumstances.

The tigers represent the people and forces controlling Men. Hanging precariously on the cliff face represents the precarious position Men hold in our society. The monk represents a Warrior who chooses to live in the moment by enjoying the strawberry rather than responding to multiple challenges.

I wrote this book for three reasons.

To **TEACH** the attributes of the Warrior Life.

To describe how to **LIVE** the Warrior Life.

And a **CALL TO ACTION** to make **TEACHING** and **LIVING** the Warrior Life our Mission.

I've talked with many Men over the years who suffer from anxiety, depression, malaise, high blood pressure, etc., and who've endured years of non-specific feelings of anger, resentment, and discontent. They're extremely frustrated with their lack of success in making a better life for themselves and many have quit trying because they are mentally, physically, and spiritually exhausted.

Our society exacerbates the problem of Cognitive Dissonance by requiring Men to place themselves in "harm's way" and/or work in physically and emotionally challenging environments while making allowances for Women who receive the same pay and benefits and who are, in many cases, promoted faster than them to meet diversity goals.

Men are never honored because they're Men whereas the media and others make it a point to highlight Women's contributions even when they are negligible. Under the guises of equality and diversity our society has forced Women into traditionally male occupations destroying their male-oriented cultures making them less satisfying to Men. Our society has given and inordinate amount of power to the "Vocal Minority" which is negatively impacting Men's' lives.

I receive resistance 100% of the time I mention that Dissonance is the source of many Men's problems and that our society exacerbates the problem. It requires significant study and thought before someone truly understands what Dissonance is and how it negatively affects the quality of Men's lives

Unfortunately, many Men are so debilitated by Dissonance that they don't have the will, support, or knowledge to make changes that would improve significantly the quality of their lives. Many Men are so beaten down they'd rather continue to live "their lives in quiet desperation" than make even the most minor changes. However, these Men shouldn't be judged negatively because most Men know only the pain of living a dissonant life having never experienced the Joys of living as Warriors.

The following chapters will **Teach** the attributes of Warriors, describe how to **Live** as Warriors and through a **Call** to **Action** motivate Men to make living the Warrior Life their Missions.

In the next chapter I'll discuss the first Attribute of being a Warrior which is a **Warrior surrounds himself with Warriors**.

Chapter I.

A Warrior Surrounds Himself with Warriors

Jeremiah 20
¹¹But the Lord stands
beside me like a great warrior.

One of the most significant epiphanies I've had occurred after having coffee with a long-time friend of mine. While driving away from our meeting I felt depressed, stressed, irritated, anxious, mad, cynical, and emotionally miserable which was completely the opposite of how I felt before our meeting. My **Epiphany** was that I didn't have to accept the negative outcomes of our friendship or even continue a relationship that

> An **epiphany** is an experience of sudden and striking realization. Generally the term is used to describe scientific breakthrough, religious or philosophical discoveries, but it can apply in any situation in which an enlightening realization allows a problem or situation to be understood from a new and deeper perspective.
>
> *Wikipedia*

was negatively impacting my life. I had a choice. I could choose to continue to associate with this Man or I could dedicate the time to **Fellowship** with a Warrior who would be a positive influence in my life. I didn't have to continue meeting with my friend just because we've known each other for years. I could end the relationship and not feel guilty because of possibly hurting his feelings or because I was braking a social obligation.

> *Fellowship is a friendly association, especially with people who share one's interests.*
> Oxford Dictionary

My former friend is a financially successful older Man who spent most of his life working his way up from the "mean streets" of northeastern cities. Although he hadn't been near a "mean street" in decades he acts as though he's still in the mix unable and unwilling to turn-off his "mean streets" attitude. He rarely has anything positive to say and is proud of his resolutely disdainful attitude.

He is especially concerned about being respected which causes significant stress and discord. There were times he'd laugh at a joke and other times he become livid about a perceived slight and get up and walk-away without saying a word. Being respected to him meant that he always had to be the center of attention, had to tell the best story, and had to have the last word. If at any time he thought he was being disrespected he'd stand-up abruptly and walk-away. His behavior made me extremely uncomfortable because his rude behavior denied others the respect he demanded and having to deal with his volatile behavior.

James 3

[12]My brothers, a fig tree cannot produce olives, nor a grapevine figs, can it? Neither can a salt spring produce fresh water.

After knowing him for over five years I realized he was never going to change and he was always going to be a negative influence in my life. I tried to get him to moderate his negative behavior with absolutely no success whatsoever. Every time I suggested he modify his behavior so others wouldn't feel so uncomfortable with him he'd counter that he was too old to change and saw no reason to. He was happy the way he was living and didn't give a damn what other people thought. The combination of a huge **Ego** and low self-esteem made him an extremely unpleasant person to be around.

Another former friend of mine is a conspiracy addict spending his life in front of his computer sending long detailed emails and writing on blogs about a plethora of topics having to do with fighting the "One World Order" and how shady insidious

> *The **Ego** is the organized, realistic part of the mind that mediates between the desires of the id and the super-ego.*
> *Wikipedia*

forces are working constantly, and unremittingly to enslave the world's population by taking over the banking systems thus gaining complete and unassailable power.

Everything he sees, hears, and reads has to do with the war between numerous crafty opponents positioned strategically throughout the world. He never lets even the hint of a conspiracy go unattended because must have a least three going on at a time or he feels sad, listless, and bored. The research, study, discussion, and exposing of conspiracies gives meaning to his life.

I tried on many occasions without success to direct our discussion away from his very paranoid psych phrenic view of life. Unfortunately, he's like many older people who needlessly suffer from a much lower quality of life because they spend many hours alone listening to or watching the News broadcast 7/24 by the mass media. Being that the mass media News is an overwhelming negative source of information it develops and maintains feelings of fear and insecurity negatively impacting peoples lives.

As a result of my epiphany I decided I'd stop spending time with my two friends and find Warriors to replace them. I also reviewed the quality of my friendships with other Men and decided who I was going to spend time with and who I was going to replace with Warriors.

This may be perceived as cold and "self-centered" but Warriors make decisions and follow through with them regardless of how difficult they may be. Warriors know the short-term negative effects of decisions are usually insignificant compared to the value of the long-term benefits and are willing to persevere.

It's very difficult to reject the company of long-time friends but sometimes that's what needs to be done. I don't expect friends to be a positive influence all of the time because only God can be that. But I do expect that over time my friendship with them will be a mutual net gain in joy, knowledge, and fellowship.

2 Thessalonians 3

³In the name of our Lord Jesus, the Messiah, we command you, brothers, to keep away from every brother who is living in idleness and not living according to the tradition that they received from us.

+——— +——— +——— +——— +——— +——— +——— +——— +——— +———

The "Narrative" that Men are being "self-centered" when they attend to themselves is a very pervasive force that **controls who** Warriors **Fellowship** with and **how** they spend their time.

I heard a recently divorced Woman complain to her friends about how horrible her ex-husband is acting now that they're divorced. She sneered "he thinks it's all about him now". I don't know the specific reasons for her divorce but I suspect it has to do with her thinking she had to have substantial control over her husband.

Hers and others attempts to control **who** her husband spent his time with prevented him from living a Warrior Life causing a marriage to end and a family broken.

Another example of how Warriors are controlled is in the choice of **how** they spend their free-time. When I grew up my father and I'd go to hunting camp in the Fall where we spent time with other Warriors resting and rejuvenating. My parents had six children so I'm sure my mother was happy to get a break from my father and me. We went to hunting camp in the Fall, ice fishing in the winter, and fresh-water fishing in the spring and summer. Throughout the year we'd go off on our own and do Manly things in Manly ways with no one thinking we were self-centered. We were doing what Men do.

Modern narratives perpetuate the idea that Men are expected to spend all of their time with their families (who) on vacations (how) at high-priced locations that are advertised prominently during Women and children's programming. If he doesn't take his family on vacation but instead spends his time with Men he's considered self-centered, cheap, and just downright mean.

So what happens is he stresses-out loading-up the family and staying in overpriced rooms eating overpriced food while attending "kid-friendly" entertainment designed to lower his status below that of his wife and children. He's kept busy all day keeping track of and protecting his family eventually going to sleep late at night mentally and physically exhausted.

Oh and don't think for a minute that he deserves any special dispensation like taking some time out of the family vacation to do something for himself. Nooooo. This is a "family vacation" so he must do everything with the family whereas as his wife, who every thinks deserves the vacation more than he does, feels perfectly justified and is encouraged to take a "mother's day out" from the family and enjoy her much deserved rest.

The results of the "family vacation" are the children are happy, mom's rested, and dad's a stressed-out mess. To be rejuvenated Warriors must spend time with other Warriors (who) in environments that are rustic and primitive in natural settings with Warriors doing Warrior-like things (how).

A significant problem with modern technology is it allows for 7/24 access to almost everyone almost anywhere forcing us to remain mentally engaged with the world whether we want to or not. Younger generations have never lived without cell phones or computers. They're minds have developed an unhealthy attachment to technology. It's considered a severe punishment if you take a cell phone or computer away from them because they've been conditioned to rely on technology to communicate and keep their minds busy. I've watched a group of high schoolers sitting around a table not talking and staring down at their telephones while texting each other. The art of face-to-face conversation is lost in younger generations along with its benefits.

It's a difficult journey when a Man decides to live like a Warrior. There are times when he'll be perceived as being selfish, rude, disrespectful, etc. but, Warriors know they must stay strong and defy the people who will try to control him. Warriors know they must take time out for themselves so they will operate at their peak in defending and supporting their families

Proverbs 27

[17]Iron sharpens iron; so a Man sharpens a friend's character.

This reminds me of an old story about a young lumberjack who decides he's going to be the new "Bull of the Woods". He heads out early in the morning determined to chop down more trees than anyone else in camp. The reigning "Bull of the Woods is an old guy lumberjack who takes his time to eat a big breakfast and sharpen his axe before heading out. He places his sharpening stone in his pocket knowing he'll need it later in the day.

As the day goes on the old lumberjack stops every once in a while to catch his breath and sharpen his axe. The young lumberjack intent on beating the old guy just keeps chopping away. Later in the day the young lumberjack is having increasing trouble chopping down trees even though he's working just as hard as when he started. The old lumberjack takes time to eat lunch, play a game of pinnacle, and sharpen his axe. Finally, at the end of the day the foreman counts the trees to see who the "Bull of the Woods" is. Unfortunately, the young lumberjack wasn't able to accompany the Men on the count because he was too exhausted. After the count it was determined that the old lumberjack had retained his title by a wide margin.

When the young lumberjack finally made his way back to the bunkhouse he collapsed on his bed exhausted. When he regained consciousness he begged the old lumberjack to tell him his secret. The old lumberjack told him that everyone has to stop now and again to sharpen their axe because if they don't it'll get duller and duller making them much less productive regardless of how hard they try. The little time the old lumberjack spent sharpening his axe and resting paid huge dividends later in the day.

The moral of the story is a Warrior knows when his axe needs sharpening and he's not dissuaded when he decides to take time to rejuvenate himself for the ongoing battle ahead. Even Jesus needed downtime and ministering.

Matthew 4

>[11]Then the devil went away, and angels came and took care of Jesus.

An angel comforting Jesus, by Carl Heinrich Bloch, 1865-1879.

I'm reminded of another story about a pair of bulls standing up on a hill looking down at a herd of cows. The young bull turns to the old bull and says, "Hey whatta say we run down there and have our way with one of them cows?" The old bull turns to the young bull and says, "How 'bout we walk down and have our way with all of 'em?"

The moral of the story is that Warriors know how to moderate their behavior so they're always ready and available to fight. Warriors don't lose battles because they're burned-out or because of short-term setbacks. Warriors are optimistic because they know God has already won the War. A Warrior knows his sacred duty is to win the ongoing battles thus protecting their families, country, and themselves against evil.

1 Thessalonians 5

>[14]We urge you, brothers, to admonish those who are idle, cheer up those who are discouraged, and help those who are weak. Be patient with everyone.

Warriors need each other for support and guidance. Without each other Warriors are left to fight evil alone making it more difficult and costly to win battles. When a Warrior fights alone it's more likely that he will succumb or quit fighting returning to the deathly slumber of his easy chair and T.V.

Ecclesiastes 4

[12]If someone attacks one of them, the two of them together will resist. Furthermore, the tri-braided cord is not soon broken.

In the next chapter I'll discuss the importance of **Warriors mastering personal protection, weapons, and being physically fit**.

Chapter II.

A Warrior Masters Personal Protection, Weapons, and is Physically Fit.

Matthew 10
**[16]You see, I am sending you out like sheep among wolves. So be
as cunning as serpents and as innocent as doves.**

A Warrior works continuously to master the knowledge and skills required to effectively protect themselves and others while maintaining an optimum level of physical fitness to the best of his abilities. The Warrior attribute of "personal protection" means the skills required to defeat an enemy using your body as a weapon for hand-to-hand fighting or by employing a variety of weapons at a wide-range of distances.

Warriors train continuously to inflict the maximum acceptable carnage upon their enemy while being completely indifferent to the smell of puke and sweat, the site of blood and guts splashed on the ground, and the feel and sound of testicles being crunched by knees thrust deeply into loins.

Give this a try. Get a rotten orange. Hold the orange in your hand. Close your eyes and place the index finger of your opposite hand on the outside of the orange. Now imagine the orange is someone's eyeball. Push your finger into the eyeball. Now remember. Did you shove your finger in all the way yelling-out a Conan the Barbarian type oath at the top of your lungs or were you squeamish and only pushed your finger in deep enough to say you did it than felt queasy afterwards and scrubbed your finger clean with hand-softening perfume smelling dish detergent that some Woman bought? I hope you were a Conan.

Numbers 1
[2](The Lord said to Moses) "From the whole community of Israel, record the names of all the warriors by their clans and families. List all the Men twenty years old or older who are able to go to war.

I'm not an expert in any specific area of personal protection however I do possess sufficient knowledge and experience to recommend general ways to improve your skills. I can't recommend any one method over another because I don't know your individual physical and mental capabilities and experiences. To get started I suggest you review respected personal protection sources, choose a method or system that meets your physical and mental capabilities, and master the system to the best of your abilities.

You should have a physical examination before you start any of the more physically demanding systems (Krav Maga) especially if you haven't been physically active. Some of you have ridden the Virtuous Cycle down as far as you can stand it and you're ready to make the changes required to climb back up. Unfortunately, some Men get caught-up in the softer-side of life causing them to become soft mentally and physically debilitated by obesity, high-blood pressure, depression, etc. The worse these conditions become the more they engage in the behavior that caused the condition in an attempt to make them feel better forcing them downward in the Cycle. The only way to move back up the Cycle is to make changes and persevere. (See Chapter VI, A Call to Action.)

I have personal experience with Krav Maga finding it to be the best system for me. I like its aggressiveness, its physicality and use of a variety of weapons, its training in mental toughness and how to operate as a "hard target", and its real-world battled-tested history of being the only "marital arts" system used by the Israel Defense Forces (IDF). Krav Maga is one of the few systems improved continuously based upon feedback received from the battlefield.

The United States Military's combatant systems are based on many of the same techniques as Krav Maga but for a number of reasons were changed slightly and renamed. I recommend you get started by researching Krav Maga and the Military's combatant systems (Army or Marines), select the system you feel an affinity for, find a qualified person to train you, and have at it.

—⊢— —⊢— —⊢— —⊢— —⊢— —⊢— —⊢— —⊢— —⊢— —⊢—

A Warrior trains continuously to master a variety of weapons. The types of weapons I'll discuss in this chapter are physical objects that are designed to function as weapons or can be used as improvised weapons to wound or kill an enemy. The second category of weapons is being mentally tough and persevering that will be discussed in the next chapter.

1 Chronicles 26

> [8]All of these sons of Obed-edom, along with their sons and brothers, were valiant Men, fully qualified for duty.

We in the great state of Texas have 2nd Amendment based laws regarding weapons to include when and where they can be carried, either concealed or open carry, and the circumstances to us "Deadly Force".

Unfortunately, many liberal governments and elected officials who have security provided by the government and/or live in gated communities with full-time security are unconstitutionally denying their citizens their God given Natural Right to defend themselves and others.

They feel free to restrict the possession and use of weapons because they and theirs are protected, they want the masses disarmed for their safety, and don't experience or live in communities with crime. They restrict ownership and confiscate weapons from law-abiding citizens even though it results in armed criminals preying on defenseless victims.

I follow all laws and regulations regarding firearms because I believe States have a duty to regulate firearms but only for public safety and restricting access by career criminals. However, there's a limit to how much regulation I'll accept. I won't compromise personal security for someone else's misguided ideas.

I've read the 2nd Amendment, know what it says, and I know our Founding Fathers' Original Intent. I've studied the 2nd Amendment and its history preventing liberal politicians and/or lawyers from manipulating its language to unconstitutionally disarm me. Even if there were no 2nd Amendment, God forbid, there is Natural Law and my sacred duty as a Warrior to know and practice weaponry to protect me and mine. The Original Intent of the 2nd Amendment was to protect citizens from the power and overreach of government. With that in mind do you think I would allow that self-same government to disarm me?

As a joke I tell people we (Texans) should coral our career criminals, we pretty much know who they are, and bus them to San Francisco where possessing firearms is illegal and where they've got a lot a money and stuff. I think our criminals would go for the deal because being a criminal in Texas is dangerous. Many Texans are armed and would shoot them happily with no hesitation whereas the San Francisco city government has disarmed their citizens predisposing them to being victims.

Admiral Hirohito, the senior Japanese military commander of WW II, said he would never consent to invading the United States because there would be an armed citizen behind every blade of grass.

Every once in a while I'll find a way to cross a weapon off my "Weapons Bucket List". For example, I want to shot a black powder rifle but I don't own a black powder rifle nor do I know much about it however I do know a Warrior that does. He knows about black powder rifles and many others so I'll use him as an opportunity to learn the mechanics and skills required to shot one accurately. (See Chapter II Warriors Surrounds Himself with other Warriors)

Finally, a Warrior's hobbies should contribute to his lethality. I've had a wide-variety of experiences and have learned that the recreational activities that hold my interest are ones that train Warriors. Examples are football, rugby, hockey, basketball, stock-car racing, hunting, fishing, orienteering, Spartan Runs,

Ninja races, Mixed Marital Arts (MAA) fighting, boxing, shooting sports of all kinds, archery, knife making and throwing, welding, black- and gun-smithing, ballistics, studying my enemies strengths and weaknesses, etc.

Limousine Liberal's rarely participate in any of the above activities making them the least knowledgeable and thus the least qualified to regulate. To stop the least qualified from having the power to regulate or lives Warriors should contribute their time and money to activities that support Warrior training. If we don't our personal security will be compromised by the least qualified who will continue to attempt to regulate something they know little about.

One should rise at four in the morning, practice sword techniques, eat one's breakfast and train with the bow, the gun and horse.
If one should require diversions, one should make them such outdoor passions as falconry, deer hunting and wrestling.
The practice of Noh [style] dancing is absolutely forbidden. When one unsheathes one sword, one has the cutting edge down keeping people in mind. As all things are born from what lies in the heart, a samurai who practices dancing, which lies outside the martial arts, should be ordered to commit hara kiri.
Having been born into the house of a warrior, one's intentions should be to take hold of a long and a short sword and die. If a man does not explore the nature of bushido every day, it will be difficult for him to die a brave and manly death.
Kato Kiyomasa, July 25, 1561 – August 2, 1611

Warriors maintain an optimum level of physical and mental fitness based on their unique strengths, weaknesses, and environments. I emphasize, **"based on their unique strengths and weaknesses"**. Every Warrior should maintain a level of physical and mental fitness that is optimized for his unique situation. In other words a 55 year-old former football linemen with bad knees can't be expected to operate at the tempo of an Active Duty Special Operations soldier. That's unrealistic. However, a Warrior should maintain a level of physical fitness so his skills and experience can be employed most effectively.

I always find it disturbingly ironic when I hear some Men talk about all the weapons they own and the ones they'd like to own; how they've taken classes in hand-to-hand combat so they're a pretty dangerous one-on-one; and how they've performed amazing feats of physical excretion yet they're currently morbidly obese with high blood pressure, diabetes, cardiovascular disease, etc.

These Men have their "War Stories" but all of the events happened in years long past. What are they doing now, today? How can they expect to survive the fight if they can't walk even short distances without wheezing? History has taught that an Army can have the best weapons in the world but they're not only useless but a hindrance if they can't be brought to bear on the enemy.

I once observed a 400+ lbs. Man crushing a chair while talking on his mobile. The Man was so fat he had no neck. He couldn't see his belly because his chin was embedded in a shelf of fat that was his chest. O.K. ya' get me? This guy was fat.

So this morbidly obese guy was lecturing someone on his mobile about proper diet, what foods were good for you and when, how the maintenance of homeostasis is improved with the correct diet, what foods should be avoided, and on and on in a very forceful and authoritative manner. I could tell he was passionate about the subject and wanted the person on the line to change their ways and improve their health. I couldn't help thinking; how could a 400+ lbs. morbidly obese Man think he could lecture someone about health and diet and be taken seriously? Unfortunately, he's like many Men who talk a good game but aren't either physically or mentally able to engage their weapons or skills in a fight.

I don't want to come off as a super-fit Warrior lecturing lesser acolytes because I'm far from it. I continue to contend with orthopedic and weight problems that I'll have for the rest of my life. However, I work continuously to be the best that I can be in whatever situation I'm in. I liked the U.S. Army slogan "Be All You Can Be" before they changed it to "An Army of One". As a side note, I never liked the Army of One slogan because I always felt a little nervous because if I'm fighting I want more than one of me in the Army. Anyways, you should be all that you can be with the mental physical gifts God has blessed you with.

I've met 90+-year-old Warriors who have problems getting around, can't see or hear so well, and are very kind and loving grandfathers who would very happily shoot you right between the eyes if you tried to hurt them or theirs. They go to the range once in a while to maintain their shooting skills and they stay active as best they can with the health God blessed them with. They're the guys you cart out front, point out the enemy, and let them have at it. They'll make every inch of ground very expensive for the enemy attriting their numbers significantly. They're Warriors because they're protecting their loved ones **to best of their abilities based on their unique strengths and weaknesses.**

In the next chapter I'll discuss why **Warriors** must be **mentally tough** and **persevere.**

Chapter III.

A Warrior is Mentally Tough and Perseveres.

Joseph 1
9"I've commanded you, haven't I? Be strong and courageous.
Don't be fearful or discouraged, because the Lord your God is
with you wherever you go."

A Warrior must be mentally tough and operate with perseverance because the battles are many and the fighters are few. A Warrior develops and maintains mental toughness by surrounding themselves with fellow Warriors, mastering personal protection and weapons, and by being physically fit. While being mentally tough a Warrior must also operate with perseverance because an inefficient, ineffective, and misdirected effort will fail causing attrition.

Deuteronomy 20
8"Let the officials also speak to the army, 'Is there a Man here
who is afraid and faint-hearted? Let him go back home.
Otherwise he may demoralize his fellow soldier.'"

By nature Warriors are optimistic with a tinge of masculine (pessimistic) humor to keep things real. I don't think a Man can be a Warrior without being an optimistic because the motivation to make things happen is energized by the belief that you will succeed. Take away the belief in success (optimism) and you'll have lower motivation and failure.

There are two reasons why I think God expects us to be optimists. First, He gave us the Gospels (Good News).

2 Thessalonians 2

[15]So then, brothers, stand firm, and cling to the traditions that you were taught by us, either by word of mouth or by our letter.

Secondly, there's no "Quit" in the bible. Believe me you won't find it I looked. NOWHERE in the bible does God tell us that we should quit. As the great Winston Churchill said in a speech in 1941 to the students at Harrow School:

"Never give in. Never give in. Never, never, never, never—in nothing, great or small, large or petty—never give in, except to convictions of honour and good sense. Never yield to force. Never yield to the apparently overwhelming might of the enemy."

Tragically, many good Christian Men have quit the fight because they didn't have the mental toughness to persevere. An example is in our schools where very few Men are teaching or involved in their governance and operation. Men involved in schools are so rare that school systems have implemented programs (i.e. Watch D.O.G.S. –Dads of Great Students) to facilitate Men spending time on campus for additional security but also to be an example for many fatherless students.

Many programs were implemented because over the years Men were pushed out of the schools and replaced with Women who are more adept at functioning within coeducational systems emphasizing activities and/or functions that are less competitive and favoring feminine characteristics.

Women and some Men who favor less competition, assertiveness, and individual achievement replaced Warriors who've traditionally been leaders in areas that play to Men's masculine gifts. Most Men don't have the mental toughness to persevere in maintaining a Warrior presence in schools resulting in schools being lead and staffed primarily by very good-hearted Woman who can't provide a balance by representing a masculine perspective.

The few Men who have toughed it out think they're challenged daily to represent masculine characteristics and interests in a system designed by and for females. They fight daily against the overwhelming feminine **Paradigm** that exists at all levels of

> *A **paradigm** is a distinct set of concepts or thought patterns, including theories, research methods, postulates, and standards for what constitutes legitimate contributions to a field.*
>
> Wikipedia

our educational systems. Unfortunately, many Men have abandoned the fight because they're discouraged and don't think fighting for career limiting ideas is worth the sacrifice.

The good news is that many leaders in our educational system have identified the problem of the absence of male models. The bad news is that we've let the absence of Men in our schools reach the point that special programs have to be established and the changes that are being made are still toeing to the feminine line. A number of times I've mentioned I don't intend to be judgmental or present myself as the perfect Warrior. Believe me I understand how difficult it is to resist overwhelming pressure to perform in a way that causes dissonance. I've been in feminine dominated environments in graduate school and in my professional career. I've experienced the frustration of trying to use more masculine oriented skills and techniques only to have them discounted and instead had to suffer through less effective more social means of getting things done.

1 James

2Consider it pure joy, my brothers, when you are involved in various trials, 3because you know that the testing of your faith produces endurance.

Being mentally tough and persevering can best be done with the advice and support of fellow Warriors. No Man is an island. Some Warriors who don't receive advice and support tend to be tough in every situation whether it's warranted and are stubbornly persistent when it is misdirected or not needed. The operative word is **"PERSEVERNCE"** which is the **Intelligent Application** of **Persistence**. Let's say I want a hole in a cement wall. I could be persistent in making a hole by head-butting the wall eventually causing brain damage and if I live long enough I may make a hole. However, that is persistence NOT perseverance. Perseverance is when you get a jackhammer and work consistently until the whole is made.

This is a good time to discuss the damage the

*Dr. Rately and Manning discuss **the process of growth and how to build resilience by inoculation against stress** in their book entitled Go Wild: Free Your Body and Mind from the Afflictions of Civilization, Little, Brown and Company, 2014 page 174. This is not just for toddlers. The evolutionary conditions that shaped us are that base of comfort and strength, the mother. Gather that strength and venture forth to explore the variety and wonder of the world, the wild. And when it jolts you, pull back, rest, and grow among people you love and trust. Whether you're stressed or relaxed, well-being is not about always being safe or fed or comfortable. Rather, it is learning to walk the line between the two, balance, to move back and forth between them with ease and grace. Well-being comes from learning to talk to the lions. The very same forces that tamed wolves and made them dogs tamed humans. Call those forces civilization, and yes, obvious and abundant benefits came with the deal. … Our bedrock point has more to do with genes, evolution, and time. Human evolution occurred under wild conditions, and this made us who we are. The modern human still operates on those same genes, almost wholly unchanged. We are designed to be wild, and by*

movie character Rambo has done too many Men. I really enjoy "Rambo: First Blood" and the follow-on movies. However, the

Rambo character has perpetuated the "Lone Wolf" myth that all Vietnam Veterans are unstable personalities living on the fringes of society biding their time too when they can finally "Release the Dogs of War" and lay waste to their communities. Rambo has also corrupted the definition of masculinity.

What's not remembered is that Rambo eventually self-destructs and goes home to his roots knowing that life is better lived with others.

Unfortunately, the **Meme** that Men need the community of other Men isn't as strong as the "Loan Wolf" meme.

> A **meme** is "an idea, behavior, or style that spreads from person to person within a culture. A meme acts as a unit for carrying cultural ideas, symbols, or practices that can be transmitted from one mind to another through writing, speech, gestures, rituals, or other imitable phenomena within a mimicked theme.
>
> Wikipedia

The "Lone Wolf" meme is reinforced constantly through Action & Adventure books and movies, of which I'm and avid fan, making people think that going it alone is an option. I've learned over the years that the most unhappy and dysfunctional Men are the "Lone Wolfs". They tend to go off on crusades that aren't, are lonely, lack a sense of direction or mission for their lives, and regardless of the negative consequences stubbornly hold onto to the erroneous belief that "Real Men" need only themselves.

In nature, which Men are much closer to than Women, you'll find that wolfs only survive and thrive in packs. The "Lone Wolf" is one that's been run out of the pack and is forced to survive on the periphery espoused to attack by other animals, starvation, and injury having to hunt alone eventually resulting in a premature and often painful lingering death. In nature, the "Lone Wolf" is a forsaken individual and is the antithesis of the much lionized Alpha Male.

One of many topics a Warrior should study is pack/herd/swarm/crowd behavior. Most species group together because at its most basic level if you're in a group you have a significantly less chance of being injured or killed than if you're alone. You also have a significantly much better chance of reproducing within the protection of a group than you do alone.

From wolfs, birds, deer, fish, people, hell even cows know it's better to be in a group than alone yet for some reason the "Lone Wolf "meme has persisted as a viable way to live.

With restrictions God allows Satan to persecute me because He knows that being challenged by and overcoming adversity is the only way I'll become closer to Him. Just as gold is purified by heating it up; I'm purified by adversity. When everything in my life is going well God recedes back into my mind. It's when I'm challenged that God moves to the front of my mind and I think to ask Him for help.

Job 23

[10]Because he knows the road on which I travel, when he had tested me, I'll come out like gold.

Warriors are mentally tough and persevere always striving to turn adversity to their advantage because regardless how dire the circumstances they know that the War is already won. They know they may lose a Battle but in the end they'll be triumphant while gaining Wisdom.

In the next chapter I'll discuss why **Warriors** must be **Wise**.

Note: Read Joseph's story in Genesis 30:24 to 50:26 to learn how a Warrior was mentally tough and persevered turning adversities into opportunities.

Chapter IV.

A Warrior Is Wise.

Ecclesiastes 7
[25]I committed myself to understand, to learn, to search for wisdom and explanations, and to understand both the evil that is foolishness and the stupidity that is delusion.

Wisdom is information applied to solving problems. A Man may know a lot of information but not be Wise because he never applies the information to solve problems, teach others, or build character. A Wise Man learns throughout his life using knowledge primarily to understand and solve problems.

Unfortunately, many Men choose not to take leadership positions or express masculine opinions because they know they are not valued for their Wisdom and will be subjected to constant pressure to conform. Theodore Roosevelt described this situation in the following excerpt from his speech "Citizenship In A Republic" speech delivered at the Sorbonne, in Paris, France on 23 April, 1910.

It is not the critic who counts; not the Man who points out how the strong man stumbles, or where the doer of deeds could have done them better. The credit belongs to the man who is actually in the arena, whose face is marred by dust and sweat and blood; who strives valiantly; who errs, who comes short again and again, because there is no effort without error and shortcoming; but who does actually strive to do the deeds; who knows great

43

enthusiasms, the great devotions; who spends himself in a worthy cause; who at the best knows in the end the triumph of high achievement, and who at the worst, if he fails, at least fails while daring greatly, so that his place shall never be with those cold and timid souls who neither know victory nor defeat.

I'm not going to address what Wisdom is in much detail because I couldn't due the subject justice. It's one of the most complicated concepts in the bible being cited in 194 verses in the International Standard Bible®.

What I'm specifically concerned with is that Warriors, especially older Warriors, are being pushed aside in favor of Women who are imbued with an **Eternal Feminine** Wisdom that isn't appropriate in all circumstances.

This is evidenced in schools where for over the last 20+ years boys have been drugged and have been the recipient of a plethora of behavioral techniques to make

*The **eternal feminine** is a psychological archetype or philosophical principle that idealizes an immutable concept of "woman". It is one component of gender essentialism, the belief that men and women have different core "essences" that cannot be altered by time or environment. The conceptual ideal was particularly vivid in the 19th century, when women were often depicted as angelic, responsible for drawing men upward on a moral and spiritual path. Among those virtues variously regarded as essentially feminine are "modesty, gracefulness, purity, delicacy, civility, compliancy, reticence, chastity, affability, [and] politeness" Wikipedia.*

them act more like girls. It's no great mystery why so many of our boys and young Men lack robustness and the character to overcome life's obstacles.

Matthew 23
[34]"That is why I am sending you prophets, wise Men, and scribes. Some of them you will kill and crucify, and some of them you will whip in your synagogues and persecute from town to town.

Men have allowed themselves to be overruled and/or discounted in many areas of our society to include child rearing, education, entertainment, popular media, sports, etc. Over the last twenty plus years Men are characterized by the popular media as incompetent, dumb, juvenile, wimpy, narcissistic, physically weak, clumsy, cowards, easily amused, dirty, etc.

The first time I noticed this was a few years ago when I saw a Hewlett Packard commercial where a little boy walks up to his father and says he needs his help because he's got to print something before he goes to school. The father looks scared and nervous and asks his son if he could wait until his mother comes home. The little boy says no he can't wait he needs the document now. The father gets up and bumbles around the house presumably looking for the computer. The little boy looks over at his father with pity then goes over to the computer and prints his document. As the little boy walks out the front door to go to school he looks back at his father who is still frantically bumbling around. His father knocks a porcelain egg onto to the floor breaking it. The little boy says to his father, "Oh boy what till mom comes home. You're going to be in trouble".

Now if a Warrior had written the commercial he would have the father tell the boy to go to school and quit bothering him. If the boy said he needed to print a document right now the father would have said Mom isn't home so it's not going to happen and he should have planned ahead and not waited to the last minute and he better do what he said and quit bothering him and GO TO SCHOOL!

There's a "**Narrative**" across all major media outlets, especially in children's and young adults' programming, that the power and influence of Men must be neutralized and at best negated for the betterment of all Mankind. In Stephen Hunter's excellent book I, Sniper he describes what a "narrative" is:

> *A **narrative** (or story) is any fictional or nonfictional report of collected events, presented in sequence of written or spoken word, or in sequence of (moving) pictures.*
>
> Wikipedia

"… the set of assumptions the press believe in, possibly without even knowing that it believes in them. It's so powerful because it's unconscious. It's not like they get together every morning and decide. 'These are the lies we tell today.' No, that would be too crude and dishonest. Rather, it's a set of casual, nonrigorous assumptions about a reality they've never really experienced that's arranged in such a way as to reinforce their importance to a system and the way they've chosen to live their lives. It's a way of arranging things a certain way that they all believe without ever really addressing carefully. It permeates their whole culture. They *know*, for example, that Bush is a moron and Obama is a saint. They *know* communism was a phony threat cooked up by right-wing cranks as a way to leverage power to the executive. They *know* Saddam didn't have weapons of mass destruction, the response to Katrina was fucked up, torture never works …Cheney's a devil, Biden's a genius. Soft power is good, hard power bad. Forgiveness excellent, punishment counterproductive, capital punishment a sin. See, Nick's fighting the narrative. He's going against the story, and the story was suspiciously concocted exactly to their prejudices, just as Jayson Blair's made-up stores and Dan Rather's Air National Guard documents were. And the narrative is the bedrock of their culture, the keystone of their faith, the alter of their church. They don't even now they're true believers, because in theory they despise the true believer in anything. But they will absolutely de-frackin'-story anybody who make them question all that…

The most common narrative portrays Men as comical, weak, ignorant, clueless, rude, physically and socially inept, yet powerful enough to subjugate Women and minorities. This narrative maintains the commonly held beliefs that Male attributes are much less valued than Women's; that we need to be kept under tight control

> In the 20th Century, "**culture**" as a central concept in anthropology, encompassing the rage of human phenome that cannot be attributed to genetic inheritance.
>
> Wikipedia

or we'll be a serious danger to society; we aren't able to take care of ourselves or others; given the chance we'd turn every room into a "Man Cave"; and that we're responsible for paying retribution for acts that we didn't personally commit. This narrative has contributed significantly to the deterioration our **Culture** for the following reasons:

———— Organizations are easily manipulated by anyone who claims to be offended. Instead of upholding traditional standards they cave in at the slightest pressure changing to meet the demands a vocal minority. The changes usually cost resources and rarely benefit the majority. An example is the preference given to Women for employment in certain jobs because they are underrepresented based on the percentage of them in the population. Although there are very few Women willing to work in construction and other physically demanding jobs employers are still required by law and commercial practices to make a concerted effort to hire them. No consideration is given to Men having to work with a Woman who is not up to standards and these Men are pressured to make allowances and go along with the program or lose their jobs.

James 3

15That kind of wisdom does not come from above. No, it is worldly, self-centered, and demonic.

———— In an effort to get along, and get girls, boys and Men have become passive. This passivity is learned through years of being told they have to repress their natural leadership abilities and work as a team regardless of how many hours are wasted. I've been in or have observed groups where everyone sits passively waiting for someone else to take the lead. When someone does indicate they're taking the lead they do it so non-assertively that the group continues to flounder due to a lack of organization and direction. The new "leader" spends an inordinate amount of time socially grooming every member in the group so they won't feel left out and the leader isn't perceived as being rude or controlling. The heartfelt need for courtesy and inclusiveness takes priority over the mission of the group. This by the way is no way to run a country or army.

Numbers 34

¹⁸You are to appoint a leader from each tribe to divide the land for inheritance.

The martial qualities that are normally second nature to boys and Men have been diluted down to where giving your kid a six-shooter to play with could be considered parental negligence requiring a family welfare visit by Family Protective Services and possible criminal charges. I remember when I was about ten-years old my father gave me my first jackknife. It was old and worn making it the perfect first knife because I couldn't mess it up more than it was. The instructions my father gave me were to be careful, don't cut myself, and keep my fingers away from the blade when closing it. After cutting my finger a couple of times I learned that the blade will snap closed whether my finger is there or not so I'd better pay attention to what I was doing. By experiencing this on my own I learned to respect knifes and other sharp and pointy objects and that a lack of attention has painful consequences.

Psalms 45

³Put on your sword,
O mighty warrior!

Traditional initiation events for boys have been negated or stopped causing many Men to never transition into adulthood and accept its responsibilities. The subject of boys' initiation rites is very interesting and complex spanning every culture worldwide with the most common way boys' are initiated is by being taken away from the Women and children; isolated either individually or in a small group sans females; physically and mentally stressed until they overcome a significant personal or group challenge; participate in a Men only initiation ceremony; than return to their families no longer a boy but a Man where they are expected to act like Men, get married, have children, and fulfill their responsibility to continue the tradition of initiation for their sons and other boys into the community. There change in status signifies to everyone that the boy is gone never to return. Traditional initiation events in the U.S. included playing football, joining the military, going hunting with Men, graduating from college, and many others. However, most of these events have been changed so much they: no longer challenge boys (required water brakes, limited physical exertion or contact fearing injuries to include the now fashionable concussion, limited and very highly supervised environmental exposure); include females either as an initiate or in leadership roles which negates the initiation (girls playing on boys teams, coeducational programs, integrating Women into basic training and active Army units, turning over leadership roles to Women because there's a feeling that it will be much safer and better for the boys); they have been made so difficult to operate that they've been stopped all together (marksmanship, knife making in shop class, archery, contact sports).

Genesis 21

> [20]God was with the boy as he grew up. He settled in the wilderness and became an expert archer.

Our nation's position in the world has been weakened significantly because while most countries operate like masculine sovereign nations the United States wants to be nice, get along, and not hurt anyone emotionally or physically and well we just don't want to be a bother to anyone. Unfortunately, the world doesn't work the way the proponents of the feminine approach to foreign relations wants it too. In most countries, especially in the Middle East, power is the primary determinant in relationships. If you're powerful they listen and may do what you want. If you're not you'll be ignored, exploited, or attacked. Might makes right. One of the many examples of a failure in feminine based foreign relations is the annexation of Crimea by Alexander Putin, President of Russia. When President Putin was asked if the annexation of Crimea was legal he said that yes of course it was. When President Obama was told that Putin said the annexation was legal he huffed, "Well he must be talking to a different team of lawyers than we are." I'm not positive but I really don't think Putin is talking to any lawyers. He's being a Man and acting in the best interests of his country regardless what lawyers, media, movie stars, talking heads, analysts, polls, etc. have to say whereas Obama is "Leading from the rear" and endangering or security. The Crimea, Syria, Iraq, Afghanistan, the beheading of American citizens, piracy, the braking and realignment of alliances, scorn heaped on us from nations we give billions of dollars to a year in foreign assistance, and many others are examples of our limited power which has allowed more powerful groups to form, take control, and challenge the United States.

Romans 9

[17]For the Scripture says about Pharaoh, "I have raised you up for this very purpose, to demonstrate my power through you and that my name might be proclaimed in all the earth."

Many boys and Men are feeling stress and anxiety because they perceive a dissonance between what they think and feel and how they're expected to act. This dissonance causes some boys and Men to feel alienated to the point that they no longer participate in society. I see many boys and Men spending an inordinate amount of time playing first-person "Shooter" video games because they feel powerless, not wanted, respected, or appreciated yet they're expected and sometimes required to make sacrifices for Women and children without even the least consideration. It used to be Men were respected and given special considerations because they were the bread winners, protectors, and may be required to sacrifice their lives for their families or country. Men are still expected to do all of that but are scorned if they express the belief that they should be allowed some preferences for their burdens. The venders of diversity and feminists would pile on excoriating them for being so prejudiced and mean spirited. The miscreant may even be required to attend classes to be reprogrammed.

Micah 2

[2]They covet fields and seize them; they covet houses, and grab them, too. They harass the valiant Man, along with his household, an individual and his estate."

Many forces have sapped the masculinity out of many boys and Men and have replaced it with femininity. There's been a trend emerging over the 10+ years of Woman wanting to know, "Where are all the Men?" Well the answer is their gone and it'll take a couple of generations to make new ones. God made Men and Women close enough to have a relationship but different enough to make it interesting. If both people in a relationship act the same than there are no differences to experience and enjoy causing feelings of depression and loss. Many Men and boys have found it's much easier to sublimate their feelings then express and act on them. In my opinion this sublimation causes anger and resentment which is released passive aggressively (not marrying, chronic unemployment, criminality, acting immature) or aggressively (school shootings, criminality, gangs,).

Genesis 2

[23]So the Man exclaimed, "At last! This is bone from my bones and flesh from my flesh. This one will be called 'Woman,' **because she was taken from Man**."

Attaining Wisdom is how Warriors combat the forces of evil. In addition to Wisdom Warriors must also be resourceful and flexible never being overwhelmed by situations regardless of how bad and/or unexpected they may be. That's a lot easier said than done but it is one of the most important characteristics that set Warriors above all others. The following classic poem If by Rudyard Kipling best describes Warriors.

> If you can keep your head when all about you
> Are losing theirs and blaming it on you;
> If you can trust yourself when all Men doubt you,
> But make allowance for their doubting too:
> If you can wait and not be tired by waiting,
> Or, being lied about, don't deal in lies,
> Or being hated don't give way to hating,
> And yet don't look too good, nor talk too wise;
> If you can dream---and not make dreams your master;
> If you can think---and not make thoughts your aim,
> If you can meet with Triumph and Disaster
> And treat those two impostors just the same:
> If you can bear to hear the truth you've spoken
> Twisted by knaves to make a trap for fools,
> Or watch the things you gave your life to, broken,

And stoop and build'em up with worn-out tools;
If you can make one heap of all your winnings
And risk it on one turn of pitch-and-toss,
And lose, and start again at your beginnings,
And never breathe a word about your loss:
If you can force your heart and nerve and sinew
To serve your turn long after they are gone,
And so hold on when there is nothing in you
Except the Will which says to them: "Hold on!"
If you can talk with crowds and keep your virtue,
Or walk with Kings---nor lose the common touch,
If neither foes nor loving friends can hurt you,
If all Men count with you, but none too much:
If you can fill the unforgiving minute
With sixty seconds' worth of distance run,
Yours is the Earth and everything that's in it,
And---which is more---you'll be a Man, my son!

Warriors are resourceful and flexible in achieving the outcomes they want. They see the "Big Picture" and stay on the path to their desired outcome. Warriors aren't caught up in "Drama" and insignificant details and do the best they can with the resources God gives them without resentment or compliant. They're also willing to sacrifice their egos and allow others to receive accolades as long as it will contribute to their desired outcome. Nothing will deter a Warrior. No matter how difficult or hopeless a situation is Warriors always fight to the best of their abilities knowing that the desired outcome is the most important thing. A Warrior is ready and willing to sacrifice for the benefit of others.

Revelation 2

[19]'I know what you've been doing—your love, faithfulness, service, and endurance—and that your last actions are greater than the first.

Unfortunately I've seen where Warriors have fought and won battles yet were pushed aside for others to benefit. I've noticed over that last 20+ years there's been a push for Women to be politicians, diplomats, police officers, military leaders, and etc. all at the expense of Men. There is a plethora of programs and resources for Woman to gain the education and experience to excel in leadership roles. However, at the end of the day it's the Warriors who are the power behind everything. Clausewitz said that War is the extension of diplomacy. Without the ability and willingness to fight a country will be negatively impacted by others more powerful or willing to fight. Women are functioning in roles that provide them the benefits of a position without having to risk their minds and bodies to maintain them. There's an old joke that I don't worry about what's going on in the world because when things get bad enough my country will come calling. They'll want me to go someplace to do something to restore our power, control a situation, provide humanitarian relief, etc. Once the crisis is over we'll be sent back to our lives and Women will retake the power until the next crisis when we'll be called to bail them out yet again.

A common narrative I've heard from Men is that Women think that Men need to stand aside because they are due the opportunity to exercise power. The following are a few examples:

For generations Men have sacrificed their lives advancing medical science and building a world-class medical system but are expected to stand-aside while Woman are appointed to powerful leadership positions.

Millions of Men have been wounded and died for our country protecting and expanding our way of life yet Men are expected to hand-over without complaint leadership roles in our stable, equalitarian, and prosperous country.

The popular media loves to showcase Women politicians talking about something or another without acknowledging the Men who have to back them up. Women politicians can pass all the laws they want but if Men aren't standing by willing to use force they are powerless.

Women in the military receive the same pay and benefits and sometimes advanced promotion over Men yet they don't serve in the same manner as Men. When a Woman becomes pregnant she's routinely given restricted duty which usually involves sitting behind a desk. When the babies born Women are given maternity leave that doesn't count against their annual 30 days leave. When a Woman on active duty becomes pregnant she's non-deployable and on restricted duty for over a year. Meanwhile Men have to be deployable at all times, perform her duties, and operate in a much less comfortable and safe environment and are expected to be supportive of a system that rewards equally for unequal service.

In law enforcement Men almost exclusively serve on Special Weapons and Tactics (SWAT), Special Response Teams (SRT), Special Operations Response Teams (SORT), etc. and is the muscle behind every apprehension and confinement.

As Warriors age they expand their experiences learning the ability and gaining the understanding to "put things in perspective", "see the big picture", "know the difficult sacrifices required and the benefits to their communities derived from being Warriors", etc. The more challenging experiences a Warrior has the more of an asset he becomes.

"Whether true or not, I have read we were the only American troops to ever come under battleship bombardment. It was a long, long time of knowing you could be in the last minute of your life. With the survival of Parris Island and that battleship bombardment I was armed for life to take all future unpleasant experiences with a philosophy of "I have survived worse". You'll be SOR-REE! By Sic Philips

In the next chapter I'll discuss why **Warriors must serve God above all else**.

Chapter V.

A Warrior Serves God Above All Else.

Matthew 22
[36]Teacher, which is the greatest commandment in the Law?
[37]Jesus told him, "You must love the Lord your God with all your heart, with all your soul, and with all you mind.
[38]This is the greatest and most important commandant".

The idea that a Warrior serves God above all else took me years to understand and accept because I was taught that family (Blood) always came first. My father used to say, "You can fight all you want in the house been when you kids step outside your family and you stick together". I had it drilled into my head that nothing takes precedence over family. Your family is everything. You're nothing without your family and once you become part of the family, either through birth or marriage, nothing will be spared to help you and no one outside the family will supersede you.

Psalms 19
[8]The precepts of the LORD are upright, making the heart rejoice. The commandment of the LORD is pure, giving light to the eyes.
It took many years of study until I understood that a Warrior serves God above all others because he knows by serving God he will most effectively serve himself, family, and community. I still have a difficult time understanding this

commandment. I think my difficulty stems from the fact that over the years I've heard of many people who became "born again" and left their families and communities to follow a person and/or religion only to find they were taken advantage of by people who used religion for emotional and/or financial gain. They ended-up either lost or returned to their families to find that they hurt them beyond repair, they felt extreme guilt and remorse for the emotional pain and lost time taking years, if ever, to renter their communities.

John 14

⁶Jesus told him, "I am the way, the truth, and the life. No one comes to the Father except through me.

After years of thought I discovered the person's problems weren't caused by following God; their problems were caused by following someone or thing other than the true God. Either they followed someone who twisted Christianity to their own lascivious ends and/or they held false beliefs that power and money were the most important things in life.

Matthew 6

²⁴"No one can serve two masters, because either he will hate one and love the other, or be loyal to one and despise the other. You cannot serve God and riches!"

³³But first be concerned about God's kingdom and his righteousness, and all of these things will be provided for you as well.

I've told many people they don't have to believe in the Christian God to receive the many benefits (blessings) of the Bible. If it makes them feel better they can think of the bible as a book of Wisdom of the ages. A book that contains all of the information they'll ever need to lead a Good life. Not necessarily a carefree life but a Good life. I've heard the bible described as a "Human User's Manual", "Human's Book for Dummies," a book of ancient myths, etc. It's not important how it's described what's important is that it's read and applied.

Proverbs 19

> [16]Whoever obeys a commandment keeps himself safe, but someone who is contemptuous in conduct will die.

The United States is a Judea-Christian country based on the precepts of Christianity enshrined in the Constitution. Our country's founders came to this continent for religious freedom. They brought the bible with them and applied it to their governments and in their daily lives. The idea that they thought there should be a separation between church and state is false. Nowhere in the Constitution does it say that. What it says is that the government will not sponsor a religion. The Founders wanted their government to be based on Christian principles. What they didn't want was their government favoring one religion over another or using religion to manipulate its citizens as the Anglican Church did in the British Empire.

The idea of separation of church and state originated in a letter Thomas Jefferson sent in 1802 to the Danbury Baptists describing the First Amendment and it's restriction on the legislative branch of the federal government.

> "...I contemplate with sovereign reverence that act of the whole American people which declared that their "legislature" should "make no law respecting an establishment of religion, or prohibiting the free exercise thereof," thus building a wall of separation between church and State."

The Danbury Baptists were a religious minority concerned about the dominance of the Congregationalist Church in Connecticut. The intent of Jefferson's letter was to assure the Danbury Baptists that the federal government wouldn't support one religion over another as the British had done with the Anglican Church (Church of England). Many Baptists experienced persecution by the British government through the use of the power granted to the Church to control and influence the population and politics.

1 Samuel 12

[14]If you fear the LORD, serve him, obey him, and don't rebel against the commandment of the LORD, then both you and the king who rules over you will truly follow the LORD your God.

Jefferson never intended nor did he imagine that our government should completely eliminate Christianity from its formation and operations. It's only in recent history that the misconception of a separation of church and state means completely illuminating Christianity from our government.

I don't know how many times I've heard someone state emphatically that the separation of church and state is in the Constitution. In every instance I've challenged them to find it. They never do because it's not there. On the contrary by following the precepts of Christianity our country's Founders established the greatest nation in the history of civilization with the unique beliefs that all Men are created equal and that the authority of the Constitution isn't derived from a King but from **Natural Law.** The source of the authority for Natural Law is God as detailed in the

> **Natural Law** *is a state of nature without government interference. Man naturally engages in certain activities in which government should not be permitted to interfere.*
> *Wikipedia*

first paragraph of the Declaration of Independence.

When in the Course of human events, it becomes necessary for one people to dissolve the political bands which have connected them with another, and to assume among the powers of the earth, the separate and equal station to which the Laws of Nature and of Nature's God entitle them, a decent respect to the opinions of mankind requires that they should declare the causes which impel them to the separation.

We hold these truths to be self-evident, that all men are created equal, that they are **endowed by their Creator** with certain unalienable Rights, that among these are Life, Liberty and the pursuit of Happiness.--That to secure these rights,

> Governments are instituted among Men, deriving their just
> powers from the consent of the governed...

In summary, our unalienable rights are derived from God. Our governments' authority is derived from us. The line of authority is God, Us, Governments. Simple.

Another discussion I've had with Atheists is that if their philosophy of life is such a good thing where are their works? Where are the hospitals, universities, schools, charities, etc.? Atheists have never built one church, university, or charitable organization of note. Throughout the world Christians have served and are serving their fellow Man in a variety of settings and ways. Christians are daily suffering and sacrificing their very lives for the benefit of their fellow Man.

Job 8

> [19]"Indeed, this is the benefit of God's way: from the soil other
> plants will sprout.

Instead of living their lives serving God many Men serve the "Unholy Trinity" of Money, Sex, and Power.

Money – is a source of happiness. The more money you have the happier you'll be. If you're not happy work harder and make or steal more money. If you're still not happy buy a big house and fill it with stuff. Buy cars, boats, motorcycles, go on many expensive vacations, etc., and if you're still not happy its' because you don't have enough money and/or you're not spending enough of it on the right things. If you're still not happy after years of working yourself nearly to death it's your fault because you have money, which should make you happy, you just don't know how to enjoy it. If all else fails use your money to pay for New Age type classes and retreats and medicate yourself with prescription drugs or pot, alcohol, crack cocaine, heroin, etc. With Money you can get more Money, Sex, and Power.

Sex – is a source of happiness. The more sex you have the happier you'll be. It's common knowledge. Look around you. There is a plethora of advertisements, shows, movies, etc., depicting how happy and satisfied people are who have a lot of sex. By the way, sex can be had with no physical or psychological consequences. Sex is an expression of our humanity so don't feel guilty it's natural. If you're not happy with the one you're with just get another. Friends with benefits are what you need and if those friends don't make you happy get others. If you feel empty and lonely have more or different types of sex. With Sex you can get more Sex, Money, and Power.

Power – is a source of happiness. They more you have the happier you'll be. The best exercise of Power is when you force others to do what you want regardless of what they want. In that way you'll have the feeling of accomplishing something after overcoming all obstacles. To be happy you must be the dominate person in every interaction and relationship. You must be the center of attention and the person who always gets their way. To be happy you must force your will on others because you are the only person who must be made happy. Your happiness is dependent on other people only to the extent that you can make them do what you want. If you're not happy go to the book store where you can buy hundreds of books that'll teach you how to gain and exercise power and will make you feel better by justifying your being ruthless in getting and keeping Power. With Power you can get more Power, Money, and Sex.

Deuteronomy 2

[14]"Now from the time we left Kadesh-barnea until we crossed the Wadi Zered was 38 years. All of that generation, the soldiers in the camp, were destroyed just as the LORD swore they would be. [15]Indeed, the hand of the LORD was against them to root them out from the camp until they were utterly destroyed." [16]"And so all the soldiers among the people died.

Men have a choice. We can live the Warrior Life using the very short-time we have on this earth building a legacy of Christian greatness or we can follow the "Holy Trinity" and spend eternity with a tarnished Legacy.

I choose the Warrior Life.
The final chapter is a **call to action.**

Chapter VI.

A Call to Action

Exodus 14
¹⁵ Then the LORD told Moses, "Why are you crying out to me? Tell the Israelis to move out!"

The proceeding chapters should give you the basic knowledge and resources to live the Warrior Life. However, you aren't a Warrior unless you apply your knowledge (Wisdom) to solve problems, help people in need, make the lives of others better, actively seek opportunities to improve and learn new skills. Warriors are active participants in all areas of their life and most importantly Warriors **get things done.**

Genesis 1
²⁸Then God blessed them and said, "Be fruitful and multiply. Fill the earth and govern it. Reign over the fish in the sea, the birds in the sky, and all the animals that scurry along the ground".

Beginning in the early sixties up to the present Men are told that they have a deep-seated possibly genetically based problem in that instead of taking the time to get in touch with their feelings and talking through their problems they insist on solving them precipitously. In other words, Men need to be more like Woman who for the most part value co-dependent relationship more than accomplishments. In other words, the pleasurable feelings of **Catharsis** and group cohesiveness are much more valued than accomplishments.

> *Catharsis* meaning "purification" or "cleansing" of emotions – especially pity and fear – or any extreme change in emotion that results in renewal and restoration.
> Wikipedia

1 John 3

> [18]Little children, we must stop expressing love merely by our words and Manner of speech; we must love also in action and in truth.

In the early 80s I attended graduate school studying psychotherapy. The dominant protocol involved "reflecting" back to the client what they said to you without being judgmental or attempting to solve their problem. I spent many hours "reflecting" which was found to be as effective as a computer that merely printed to a screen a reformatted statement of what the client typed in. Unfortunately, this protocol is still in effect in secular as well as Christian based counseling for many reasons with a dominate one being avoiding liability for a client's actions and outcomes if they actively solve their problems rather than just talking about them. If all you do is "reflect" you limit your liability and also lengthen the therapeutic process realizing higher billings.

Another reason for the longevity and prevalence of the "reflective" protocol is that it's thought, and is valid only in extremely rare cases, that if someone talks-out their problems they'll feel better even though they may not actually solve their problems. In other words it may be a better strategy to experience the positive feelings of a catharsis then the benefits of a problem solved.

When I was in graduate school there was a comic passed around, we didn't have email then, showing a client sitting with a therapist. The client tells the therapist that he's really unhappy. The therapist says, "So I hear you saying you're unhappy." The client says yes. The therapists and client sit in silence looking at each other. The client says, "I feel like getting up and jumping out that window". The therapist parrots back, "So I hear you say you feel like getting up and jumping out that window". The client walks over to the window and says, "I'm going to jump". The therapist says, "So I hear you saying you're going to jump". The client jumps out the window and screams "Ahhhhhhh.... The therapist says, "So I hear you say Ahhhhhhh.... splat".

Ecclesiastes 11
⁴He that observeth the wind shall not sow; and he that regardeth the clouds shall not reap.

In a study published in <u>Psychological Science in the Public Interest</u>, Volume 4, Number 2, November 2003 titled "Does Early Psychological Intervention Promote Recovery from Posttraumatic Stress" the authors studied the activities of 9,000 counselors who offered aid to rescue workers, families, and direct victims of violence from the attacks on the World Trade Center on September 11, 2001. Their goal was to mitigate psychological distress and prevent the emergence of Posttraumatic Stress Disorder (PTSD) using catharsis and debriefing protocols. In summary the study found:

> Psychological debriefing—the most widely used method---has undergone increasing empirical scrutiny, and the results have been disappointing. Although the majority of debriefed survivors describe the experience as helpful, there is no convincing evidence that debriefing reduces the incidence of PTSD, and some controlled studies suggest that it may impede natural recovery from trauma. Most studies show that individuals who receive debriefing fare no better than those who do not receive debriefing.

The finding that talking about traumatic events has no better outcomes than not talking is counterintuitive to most people raised in our "worried well" society. We've been erroneously told for years that we must talk about traumatic events/problems (catharsis) before their negative affects could be ameliorated or solved. Unfortunately, the more feminine talking approach takes precedence over and in many cases excludes the more masculine approach of actively solving problems and/or moving on, which may be a more successful.

1 Peter 1
[13]Therefore, prepare your minds for action, keep a clear head, and set your hope completely on the grace to be given you when Jesus, the Messiah, is revealed.

I discussed In Chapter I. (A Warrior Surrounds Himself with Warriors) how important it is for Warriors to surround themselves with Warriors. It's especially important because a Warrior gets things done by identifying and solving problems. To do this efficiently and effectively a Warrior needs someone who shares their morals and ethics, who'll hear them, give feedback, and if required tell them when it's time to quit dwelling and move on. A Warrior will also tell them if they think he needs professional help and will ensure he receives it.

A Warrior needs professional help if they're suicidal, addicted, perform or think about inappropriate or criminal behavior, are inappropriately physically violent, and a variety of other problems that may be deeply rooted and/or negatively affect themselves, families, or their communities. Warriors help Warriors solve the problems of living. They don't cover-up problems or make excuses for allowing destructive behaviors to continue.

2 James
[14]What good does it do, my brothers, if someone claims to have faith but does not prove it with actions? This kind of faith cannot save him, can it?

The reason the popular media and others feel free to disparage Men is that we've let them. The current "narrative" is that throughout history Women and children have been downtrodden by Men so it's their turn to take control completely ignoring or discounting the fact that it was overwhelmingly Men who literally paid for our relatively secure and prosperous country with their blood, sweat, tears, and the ultimate sacrifice of their lives.

The liberal media has gradually and surreptitiously changed the purpose of popular media from primarily entertainment to social programming. Journalists in the 1970s thought of themselves as advocates and activists, which continues to today, and modeled themselves after Carl Bernstein and Bob Woodward who rightfully brought-down the Nixon Presidency. However, instead of reporting the facts as they used to modern media personalities hold a position then "spin" the facts and their reporting to support their position regardless of the Truth.

Beginning in the early 80s the bad guys in movies was the government and/or military. The plot of many popular movies was that the liberal free-thinker sometimes journalist or scientist bravely stood against Men in the government/military or CIA, etc., to save defenseless and ignorant people from their nefarious activities that was leading to a disaster of some kind. Portraying the government/military as the bad guy changed in the late nineties because the theme was worn out but also it was difficult to continue to make the government/military the bad guy when soldiers were dying in wars.

The shift to disparaging Men across the majority of media platforms begin primarily with commercials, and since there was no liberal outcry bled into other forms of media. Movies depicted Women as able or more able then Men to perform martial techniques to include strategy and tactics and they could be just as physical and ruthless as Men.

I can think of two examples of many that stand-out where liberals have used the media to "socially program". The first example is the characters Angelina Jolie's plays in her movies. In the movie <u>Salt</u> she single handily kills or severely wounds a platoon-sized element of Men in a hallway. She flips, spins, kicks, punches, etc. dispatching assailants who were depicted as well-trained military-type Men. Another movie of hers was <u>Lara Croft: Tomb Raider</u> where she's portrayed as more competent than Men functioning in what was considered a traditionally male role. I know movies are fiction but if you experience fiction enough, especially the young, it's eventually assumed to be reality. Remember, Joseph Goebels, the Nazi Reich Minister of Propaganda, said if you repeat a lie enough times it becomes the Truth.

The second example is in the first Jurassic Park movie where the character playing the billionaire philanthropist responsible for founding the park tells the Laura Dern character that he was concerned about her safety. She turns to him as says something like "when we have time we'll discuss the efficacy of Women in disaster situations". The statement was a blatant attempt to establish the idea that Women are just as or more effective in emergency situations the Men. Her line was delivered in a sarcastic manner as though the stupid Man just didn't get it. He was living in the past and needed to catch-up.

The Truth is there are some Women who are as or more effective than Men in disaster situations but it's my experience that they are a very small minority. However, that doesn't hinder private and government organizations from putting Women in traditionally male roles and promoting them to higher levels of responsibility while showcasing them as representative of the vast majority of Women. For example, Women make-up about 15% of the military yet when you see Presidents giving a speeches their backdrops are comprised of over thirty percent Women giving the subliminal message that they're more numerous than they are in fact. This sustains and propagates the narrative that Women are a vital component of our military and that they serve as equals to Men. I agree Women are a vital component of our military but I know from first-hand experience that they do not serve in the same capacity of Men. They serve in less physically taxing and dangerous support roles whereas Men comprise 100% of our combat arms whose mission is to locate and destroy our enemies.

Many times I've talked to people who have no experience with the military yet they will expound on the belief that Women are equal to Men in every capacity. Of course they'll never have to risk their or their loved-ones lives fighting our enemies who have no such liberal views. The only equal opportunity in War is death.

Isaiah 5
[28]Their arrows are sharp, all their bows ready for action. Their horses' hooves seem like flint, and their chariot wheels spin like a whirlwind.

I don't want it to seem that I'm disparaging Women and their service to our country. They serve and die just as Men do however not nearly as often or in the same challenging environments. We need to be realistic about Women's military service so Men are not placed at a higher-risk of injury and/or death to support a fictitious narrative.

―――――――――――――――――――――――――――――――

This final chapter is a "Call to Action" because as I've written Men aren't Warriors unless they're active in solving problems especially when they're serious and deep-rooted. It's extremely challenging for Warriors to resist the extreme and pervasive pressure to conform to the prevailing feminist paradigm that is reinforced constantly by the popular media.

Revelation 12

[7]Then a war broke out in heaven. Michael and his angels fought with the dragon, and the dragon and its angels fought back. (And lost.)

I know counteracting the media's influence is extremely difficult because I've spent years doing it. Every time I watch a movie or show with my young daughter I have to explain to her that Men don't act the way they're depicted. She says she knows because she knows me but there are millions of children learning what Men are like by watching the popular media where Men are usually skinny, weak, scared, co-dependent, dumb, physically inept, and secondary to a female who is really the main character in the story. Millions of children are being socialized to think that Men are at best not necessary and at worst inept.

There's also the "So what" narrative that's been around for a years. This narrative goes something like "Who cares if Men are disadvantaged? They've had it so good for so many years now its "Women's time." My response is "What would happen if there was a War and no Men showed-up?" Men are suffering from a severe cognitive dissonance because they've been subjected to overt and covert pressure to conform to a world whose paradigm is the Eternal Feminine Matrix and they've been and are being disadvantaged for the sole reason of their being born a male.

My main concern is existential in that someday Men may decide that they have such an insignificant stake in their country that they chose not to risk their lives defending it. What would happen Men decided that fighting and dying for their country is just not worth it? Who would defend our country? Gloria Steinem, Nancy Pelosi, Barbara Boxer, Hillary Clinton, etc.?

Matthew 21

[12]Then Jesus went into the Temple, threw out everyone who was selling and buying in the Temple, and overturned the moneychangers' tables and the chairs of those who sold doves. [13]He told them, "It is written, 'My house is to be called a house of prayer,' but you are turning it into a hideout for bandits!" [15]But when the high priests and the scribes saw the amazing things that he had done and the children shouting in the Temple, "Hosanna to the Son of David," they became furious (and started planning to kill him).

―――――――――――――――――――――――――――――――――

Another battle that Warriors fight involves the pervasive and extremely negative effects of implementing the **Tabla Rasa** idea regarding how a person's gender identify is formed. Tabla Rasa is the idea that a human's mind is like a blank slate and that society figuratively writes on this slate the psychological characteristics we want the person to have and how we want them to act.

> *Tabula rasa refers to the epistemological idea that individuals are born without built-in mental content and that therefore all knowledge comes from experience or perception.*
> *Wikipedia*

For example, if the person is a male we force him to play with trucks, etc. teaching him to be masculine and if the person is a girl we force her to play with dolls, etc. teaching her femininity. The core concept is that society teaches the child how to act discounting any natural or genetic influences. So if you want a boy to be feminine have him play with dolls, etc. and if you want a girl to be masculine you have her play with trucks, etc. Fortunately, Tabla Rasa has been definitely disproved and is only kept alive because it is a significant idea in history and it has its backers in the liberal intellectual community. However, with that said, the Tabla Rasa idea still has significant influence over many areas of our society causing an untold amount of waste of resources and weakening of the fabric of society.

It's the Truth that boys and girls are different and are born with Natural characteristics that are imprinted on them when they were created by God. I think God instills the Warrior Attributes into a Man and facilitates his development by putting him in situations where the attributes are developed and expressed. For example, I don't think God gives us courage but puts us in situations where we have to be courageous. I don't think God gives us joy and happiness but gives us the **Free Will** to choose to be joyful or happy. I don't think God gives us love but allows us to choose to have an open heart allowing for loving relationships.

> *Free will* is the ability to choose between different possible courses of action.
> Wikipedia

Since God has given us life and all its blessings we have an obligation to fight against anything that detracts from His way. Fulfilling this obligation is why Men must know and develop continually their Warrior attributes and by which they derive their authority to act. This obligation compels Men to act because without action the War will be lost.

As Warriors we must never be concerned if we should act because God has given us the authority to act or how we should act because God will provide us with everything we'll need to win. If we must inspire; God will provide us with the words to inspire. If we must persevere; God will provide us the mental and physical strength and endurance to do so.

Warriors also must never be concerned with losing a battle because the War has already been won. Warriors know their lives are relatively short so they don't waste any of it being apprehensive or worried about fighting a battle in a War that's already won.

Revelation 22

[12]"See! I am coming soon! My reward is with me to repay everyone according to his action.

Unfortunately, many Men don't get into the fight because they don't know what they're **fighting against** (enemy) or **how to fight** (strategy and tactics).

What to Fight Against

The following is a list of false narratives that Men must actively fight against.

- Men cause most of the World's problems.
- Men must make restitution for causing problems.
- Men must be controlled or society will deteriorate leading to anarchy and exploitation of the weak.
- Men must be supervised closely because they can't take care of themselves, Women, or children.
- Women can serve successfully in all male roles.
- The cost of making changes for Women is worth the benefit.
- Changes should be made regardless of the cost and negative effects on Men and society.
- All male dominated roles in society should be changed to make allowances for Women.
- Women dominated roles in society are uniquely valuable so they should be protected from the intrusion of Men.
- Men should agree with and not hesitate to accept and support changes regardless of their effects.
- The tyranny of the minority is a good thing because it prevents and compensates for injustices.
- Women should be in charge in all circumstances because they are more feeling and inclusive which is always a good thing.

One of the most disturbing and frustrating conversations I've heard in the media recently plays-out some of the above Narratives. In summary, participates were expressing their very serious concern with the fact that only about ten percent of information systems professionals are Women. They thought this was a very "serious problem" because:

———The percentage of Women in the profession should at least meet or exceed their representation in the general population regardless of their aptitude or desire to be in the profession.

———Women "feel" the industry and profession isn't culturally or structurally "Women Friendly".

———There needs to be significant changes made to the culture and structure of the profession and industry to make them more acceptable to Women.

———We are being very short-sighted because we aren't willing to bare the initial significant cost of the changes and disruption to the profession and industry which would be insignificant compared to benefits derived from the increase of Women.

How to Fight

It was obvious that not one of the participates in the conversation were Warriors because if they were they would have fought by responding that it would be much more efficient, effective, and much less costly if Women adapted to the industry:

———Because the profession and industry with its current culture and structure has generated literally trillions of dollars of value for millions of people worldwide.

———The cost and disruption are real whereas the benefits are only speculative.

———90% of the people in the industry and profession seem to function adequately.

———There are no compelling reasons to change the profession and industry other than compensating for a group who have failed to adapt. Using the same logic we should also change the professions and industries of nurses (91.1% women), elementary and middle school teachers (81.8%), social workers (80.8%), meeting and convention planners (78.8%), medical and health services planners (72.5%), etc.

The above is a basic yet effective structure for acting and an example of how a cause can be fought. Warriors must identify similar situations and start battles where they stand. Because if they don't many lives will be ruined or not lived to their full potential. To assist in this effort I've included in the back of this book Scripture References and Warrior Resources to assist in the effort.

In summary a Warrior:

1. surrounds himself with Warriors.
2. masters personal protection, weapons, and is physically fit.
3. is mentally tough and perseveres.
4. is wise.
5. serves God above all else.

You no longer have an excuse to sit back and do nothing. ACT!

Author's Note

I felt compelled to write about God being a Warrior for many years but was too busy with life and other projects. The time never seemed right and I was hesitant about getting started knowing how much agony I would suffer just researching and developing a succinct list of Warrior Attributes.

The first breakthrough came when I downloaded eSword software and discovered how simple it is to use and powerful. Literally hours of research is performed in minutes with the overwhelming majority of time spent on deciding keywords to search, etc. The computer took seconds to complete what would normally take days.

The second breakthrough happened one night when I was minding my own business reading my Life Application Study Bible, New Living Translation, Second Edition, Tyndale House Publishers, Inc., www.tyndale.com and came upon the study note to the 1 Chronicles 12:1 scripture passage:

> 12:1ff David surrounded himself with great warriors, the best of the Israelite army. What qualities made them worthy to be David's warriors and servants? (1) They practiced long and hard to perfect their skills (with bow, sling, and spear); (2) they were mentally tough and determined ("fierce as lions,"12:8); (3) they were physically in shape ("as swift as deer," 12:8); (4) they were dedicated to serving God and David...

After reading the note I realized that much of the research for this book was already done. I no longer had to spend countless hours re-reading scripture to find out what God and Warriors had in common. The study note gave me and excellent summary of the information I needed to get started. After reading the note I knew that I couldn't put off writing any longer. I thought that God had given me the inspiration, tools, skills, time, information, and audience to write this book. After making modifications and expanding on the list of Attributes listed in the study note I was prepared to write.

I answered God's Call to Action and this book is the result.

Additional Scripture

Preface

Exodus 14:14 "The LORD will fight for you while you keep still."

Jeremiah 20:11 But the LORD is with me like a fearsome warrior. Therefore, those who pursue me will stumble and won't prevail. They'll be put to great shame, when they don't succeed. Their everlasting disgrace won't be forgotten.

Deuteronomy 3:18 "Then I commanded you at that time, 'The Lord your God gave you this land as a possession. Those equipped for battle—every Man a warrior—will cross before your fellow Israelis.

Deuteronomy 10:11 So the LORD told me, 'Get up and proceed to lead the people, so they may enter and take possession of the land that I promised to give their ancestors by an oath.'"

Judges 5:30 'They're busy finding and dividing the war booty, aren't they? A girl or two for each valiant warrior, and some dyed materials for Sisera—perhaps dyed, embroidered war booty—or some detailed embroidery for my neck as the booty of war!

Judges 6:12 The angel of the LORD appeared to him and told him, "The LORD is with you, you valiant warrior!"

1 Samuel 14:52 There was intense fighting against the Philistines during Saul's entire reign, and whenever Saul discovered a strong or valiant warrior, he would enlist him for service.

1 Samuel 17:33 Saul told David, "You can't go against this Philistine and fight him. You are only a young Man, but he has been a warrior since his youth."

2 Samuel 17:8 "You know how strong your father and his Men are. They're as mad as a bear robbed of her cubs! Furthermore, your father is a skilled warrior. He won't stay with his army at night.

2 Samuel 18:11 Joab asked the Man who was reporting to him, "What! You saw him? Why didn't you kill him right then and there? I would've given you ten pieces of silver and a warrior's sash!"

Job 16:14 Attack follows attack as he breaks through my defenses! He runs over me like a mighty warrior.

Psalms 45:3 Strap your sword to your side, mighty warrior, along with your honor and majesty.

Psalms 76

> 5Our boldest enemies
>   have been plundered.
> They lie before us in the
>   sleep of death.
>   No warrior could left a hand
>   against us.
>   6A blast of your
>   breath, O God of
>   Jacob,
>   Their horses and chariots
>   lay still.
>   7No wonder you are
>   greatly feared.
> Who can stand before you
>   when your anger explodes?
>   8From heaven you
>   sentenced your
>   enemies.
> the earth tumbled and
>   stood silent before
>   you.
>   9You stand up to judge
>   those who do evil,
>   O God,
> and to rescue the oppressed from this earth.
>   10HuMan defiance only
>   enhances your glory,
> for you use it as a weapon.

Psalms 78:65 The LORD awoke as though from sleep, like a mighty warrior stimulated by wine.

Psalms 89:19 You spoke to your faithful ones through a vision: "I will set a helper over a warrior. I will raise up a chosen one from the people.

Psalms 120:4 Like a sharp arrow from a warrior, along with fiery coals from juniper trees!

Psalms 127:4 As arrows in the hand of a warrior, so also are children born during one's youth.

Proverbs 16:32 Whoever controls his temper is better than a warrior, and anyone who has control of his spirit is better than someone who captures a city.

Ecclesiastes 3

> ¹For everything there is a
>   season,
>   ³A time to kill and
>   a time to heal
>   A time to tear down and a
>   time to build up
>   . . .
>   ⁸A time to love and a time
>   to hate.
>   A time for war and a time
>   for peace.

Isaiah 3:2 the mighty Man and the warrior, the judge and the prophet, the fortune-teller and the elder,

Isaiah 42:13 The LORD marches out like a warrior; he stirs up his rage like a Man of war; he makes his anger heard; he shouts aloud; he declares his mastery over his enemies:

Jerimiah 20:11 But the LORD is with me like a fearsome warrior. Therefore, those who pursue me will stumble and won't prevail. They'll be put to great shame, when they don't succeed. Their everlasting disgrace won't be forgotten.

Jerimiah 46:12 The nations have heard of your disgrace, and your cry of distress fills the earth. Indeed, one warrior stumbles over another, and both of them fall down together."

Jerimiah 50:9 Indeed, I'm going to stir up and bring against Babylon a great company of nations from the land of the north. They'll deploy for battle against her, and from there she will be captured. Their arrows will be like a skilled warrior; they won't miss their targets.

Ezekiel 3:27 "They won't be buried with dead warriors from ancient times, who went straight to Sheol, buried with their war weapons, with their swords placed under their heads and their shields laid on top of their bones, since they spread terror throughout the land of the living.

Ezekiel 39:20 You'll be fully satiated at my table, dining on horse flesh, horsemen, elite soldiers, and every kind of warrior," declares the Lord GOD.

Amos 2:14 So the swift runner will not escape, the valiant will not fortify his strength, and the mighty warrior will not save his life.

Zechariah 9:13 For I have bent Judah as if it were my bow, loading it with Ephraim. I raised up your sons, Zion, against your sons, Greece, wielding you like a mighty warrior's sword.

Matthew 10:34 "Do not think that I came to bring peace on earth. I did not come to bring peace but a sword!

Chapter I.

A Warrior Surrounds Himself with Warriors

Leviticus 25:35 If your relative becomes poor so that he is indebted to you, then you are to support him. You are to let him live with you just like the resident alien and the traveler.

2 Samuel 10:11 He said, "If the Arameans prove too strong for me, then you are to help me. If the Ammonites prove too strong for you, then I will come help you.

2 Samuel 19:14 By doing things like this, he persuaded all the Men of Judah to unite in support of him. They sent the king this message: "Come on back, you and all of your army!"

2 Samuel 22:3 He is my God, my strong stone—in him I will find my refuge—my shield, the strength of my salvation, my high tower, my way of escape, and the one who is saving me. You will save me from violence.

2 Samuel 22:19 They confronted me when I was in trouble, but the LORD remained my support!

1 Kings 1:7 He had the support of Zeruiah's son Joab and of Abiathar the priest, who followed Adonijah and assisted him,

2 Chronicles 13:7 Useless troublemakers soon gathered around him, who turned out to be too strong for Rehoboam, because he was young, timid, and unable to withstand them.

2 Chronicles 16:9 The LORD's eyes keep on roaming throughout the earth, looking for those whose hearts completely belong to him, so that he may strongly support them.

Psalms 16:5 The LORD is my inheritance and my cup; you support my lot.

Psalms 18:18 They confronted me in the day of my calamity, but the LORD was my support.

Psalms 80:17 May you support the Man at your right hand; the son of Man whom you have raised for yourself.

Proverbs 27:17 Iron sharpens iron; so a Man sharpens a friend's character.

Ecclesiastes 4:12 If someone attacks one of them, the two of them together will resist. Furthermore, the tri-braided cord is not soon broken.

Isaiah 42:1 "Here is my servant, whom I support, my chosen one, in whom I delight. I've placed my Spirit upon him; and he'll deliver his justice throughout the world.

Isaiah 63:5 I looked, but there was no helper, I was appalled that there was no one to give support; so my own arm brought me victory, and as for my wrath, it supported me.

Acts 20:34 You yourselves know that I worked with my own hands to support myself and those who were with me.

1 Peter 5:9 Resist him and be firm in the faith, because you know that your brothers throughout the world are undergoing the same kinds of suffering.

1 Peter 5:10 After you have suffered for a little while, the God of all grace, who called you by the Messiah Jesus to his eternal glory, will restore you, establish you, strengthen you, and support you.

3 John 1:8 Therefore, we ought to support such people so that we can become genuine helpers with them.

Matthew 14:30 But when he noticed the strong wind, he was frightened. As he began to sink, he shouted, "Lord, save me!"

Chapter II.

A Warrior Masters Personal Protection, Weapons, and is Physically Fit.

Numbers 1:2 "Take a census of the entire Israeli community, numbering them by their tribes and by ancestral houses. List the names of every male one-by-one, 3 from 20 years and upward. You and Aaron are to register everyone in Israel who is able to go to war, company by company.

2 Samuel 22:31 This God! His way is perfect! What the LORD declares proves true. He shields everyone who flees for protection to him!

Psalms 141:8 Nevertheless, my eyes are on you, Lord GOD, as I seek protection in you. Don't leave me defenseless!

Ecclesiastes 7:12 Indeed, wisdom gives protection, just like money does, but it's better to know that wisdom gives life, to those who have mastered it.

Genesis 27:3 so go find your weapons, take your bow and arrows, go outside, and hunt some game for me.

Judges 18:11 So 600 descendants of Dan from Zorah and Eshtaol set out for battle, armed with military weapons.

Judges 18:16 While the 600 Danite soldiers, armed with military weapons, stood guard at the entrance to the gate,

Judges 18:17 the five Men who had gone to scout out the land arrived, entered Micah's home and took possession of the carved image, the ephod, the household idols, and the cast image. Meanwhile, the priest stood outside by the entrance to the gate with the 600 Men armed with military weapons.

1 Samuel 17:54 David took the Philistine's head and brought it to Jerusalem, but he put Goliath's weapons in his tent.

1 Samuel 21:8 David told Ahimelech, "Is there no spear or sword available here? I took neither my sword nor my weapons with me, because the king's mission is urgent."

1 Samuel 31:9 They cut off his head and stripped him of his weapons. They sent people throughout the territory of the Philistines to report the good news in the temples of their idols and to the people.

1 Samuel 31:10 They put Saul's weapons in the temple of Asherah and fastened his corpse to the wall of Beth-shan.

2 Samuel 1:27 How the valiant have fallen! How the weapons of war are destroyed!"

2 Samuel 22:18 He rescued me from my strong enemy—from those who continually hate me, since they were stronger than I.

2 Samuel 23:10 but Eleazar remained standing right where he was and fought so hard against the Philistines that he became exhausted—he couldn't even let go of his sword! The LORD magnificently delivered them that day. After Eleazar had won the battle, the other soldiers returned, but only to strip the weapons and armor from the dead.

2 Kings 11:8 guarding the king and surrounding him with weapons in hand. Whoever comes within range is to be killed. Stay with the king wherever he goes, coming or going."

2 Kings 11:11 So the guards stood assembled, every soldier with weapons in hand, surrounding the king from the right side corner of the Temple to the left side corner, including around the altar and the Temple.

1 Chronicles 19:12 He told Abishai, "If the Arameans prove too strong for me, then you are to help me. If the Ammonites prove too strong for you, then I will help you.

2 Chronicles 23:7 The descendants of Levi will surround the king, brandishing weapons in their hands, and anybody who enters the Temple will be killed. Stay near the king wherever he enters and leaves."

2 Chronicles 23:10 He set the rest of the people to serve as guards for the king, and each one brandished weapons in his hand, from the south side of the Temple to the north side of the Temple, around the altar, and surrounding the palace.

2 Chronicles 32:5 Hezekiah took courage and rebuilt all of the walls that had been broken down. Then he erected watch towers on them, and added another external wall. He fortified the terrace ramparts in the city of David and prepared a large number of weapons and shields.

Job 39:21 He paws the ground in the valley and rejoices in his strength; he goes out to face weapons.

Psalms 7:13 He prepares weapons of death for himself, he makes his arrows into fiery shafts.

Psalms 76:3 There he shattered sharp arrows, shields, swords, and weapons of war.

Song of Solomon 4:4 Your neck is like the tower of David, built with rows of stones. A thousand shields are hung upon it, all the weapons of the warriors.

Isaiah 13:5 They're coming from a faraway land, from the distant horizon—the LORD and the weapons of his anger—to destroy the entire land."

Jerimiah 21:4 ʿThis is what the LORD God of Israel says: "I'm about to turn against you the weapons of war that are in your hands and with which you are fighting the king of Babylon and the Chaldeans who are besieging you outside the walls. I'll gather them into the center of this city.

Jerimiah 22:7 I'll appoint people to destroy you, Men with their weapons. They'll cut down some of your choice cedars and throw them into the fire.

Jerimiah 50:25 The LORD will open his armory, and bring out the weapons of his anger. Indeed, a work of the Lord GOD of the Heavenly Armies will be in the land of the Chaldeans.

Jerimiah 51:20 "You are my war-club and weapons of war. I'll smash nations with you and destroy kingdoms with you.

Ezekiel 23:24 "'They'll invade you with weapons, chariots, wagons, and a vast army. They'll set themselves in place to attack you from every direction with large shields, small shields, and helmet. I'll turn over judgment to them, and they'll punish you according to their own standards.

Ezekiel 32:12 I'm going to make your gangs die using the weapons of valiant warriors, all of whom are ruthless people. They will devastate the majesty of Egypt, destroying all of its hordes.

Ezekiel 32:27 "They won't be buried with dead warriors from ancient times, who went straight to Sheol, buried with their war weapons, with their swords placed under their heads and their shields laid on top of their bones, since they spread terror throughout the land of the living.

Ezekiel 33:26 You keep trusting in your weapons, you continue to commit loathsome deeds, Men keep defiling their neighbors' wives, and you're going to take possession of the land?

Ezekiel 39:9 "After all this happens, the people who live in the cities of Israel will be kindling fires for seven years, using small shields, large shields, bows, arrows, clubs, personal weapons, and spears to do so.

Ezekiel 39:10 They won't need to cut down trees from the fields nor gather firewood from the forests, because they will light fires with the weapons as they plunder the plunderers and loot the looters!" declares the Lord GOD.

Zechariah 9:10 I will banish chariots from Ephraim and horses from Jerusalem. War weapons will be banished, and your king will speak peace to the nations. His dominion will extend from sea to sea, and from the River to the farthest portion of the earth.

John 18:3 So Judas took a detachment of soldiers and some officers from the high priests and the Pharisees and went there with lanterns, torches, and weapons.

2 Corinthians 10:4 For the weapons of our warfare are not those of the world. Instead, they have the power of God to demolish fortresses. We tear down arguments.

Luke 12:40 So be ready, because the Son of Man is coming at a time when you don't expect him."

Luke 19:43 because the days will come when your enemies will build walls around you, surround you, and close you in on every side.

Chapter III.

A Warrior Is Mentally Tough and Perseveres.

Genesis 19:13 because we're going to destroy it. The LORD knows how their behavior stinks, so he sent us here to destroy it!

Deuteronomy 31:29 because I know that after my death, you'll surely act wickedly and turn from the road that I've instructed you. As a result, evil will fall on you in days to come, because you'll act wickedly in the sight of the LORD, causing him to become angry due to your behavior."

1 Chronicles 21:7 God considered this behavior to be evil, so he attacked Israel.

Ezra 9:13 "After all that has happened to us because of our evil behavior, and because of our great sin—considering that you our God have punished us less than our iniquities deserve and have given us this deliverance—

Job 23:10 Because he knows the road on which I travel, when he had tested me, I'll come out like gold.

Job 34:11 because he repays a person for his behavior; and according to a person's conduct, he lets it happen to him.

Job 34:21 Yes, Job, his eyes constantly watch the behavior of human beings; he carefully observes their every step.

Job 34:25 Thus he acknowledges their behavior, and overcomes them; when night time comes, they are crushed.

Psalms 119:9 Bet. How can a young Man keep his behavior pure? By guarding it in accordance with your word.

Proverbs 1:3 for acquiring the discipline that produces wise behavior, righteousness, justice, and upright living;

Proverbs 7:25 Don't be led astray by her lifestyle, and don't imitate her behavior.

Proverbs 14:14 The faithless one will pay for his behavior, but a good Man will be rewarded for his.

Proverbs 21:8 The conduct of a guilty Man is perverse, but the behavior of the pure is upright.

Isaiah 1:16 "Wash yourselves, and make yourselves clean; remove your evil behavior from my presence; stop practicing what is evil.

Isaiah 48:10 Look, I have refined you, but not like silver; I have purified you in the furnace of affliction.

Jeremiah 13:27 I've seen your detestable behavior: your adulteries, your passionate neighing, your lewd immorality on the hills in the field. How terrible it will be for you, Jerusalem! You are unclean. How much longer will this go on?"

Jeremiah 35:15 I've sent you all my servants, the prophets, sending them again and again. I've said, 'Each of you turn from his evil behavior and make your deeds right. Don't follow other gods to serve them. Then you will remain in the land that I gave to you and to your ancestors. But you haven't paid attention and you haven't obeyed me.

Ezekiel 3:18 "So when I say to a wicked person, 'You're about to die,' if you don't warn or instruct that wicked person that his behavior is wicked so he can live, that wicked person will die in his sin, but I'll hold you responsible for his death.

Ezekiel 3:19 If you warn the wicked person, and he doesn't repent of his wickedness or of his wicked behavior, he'll die in his sin, but you will have saved your own life."

Ezekiel 5:9 In fact, I'm going to do what I've never done before and what I'll never again do, because of all of your loathsome behavior:

Ezekiel 7:8 "Very soon now, I'll pour out my burning anger on you. I'll complete expressing my anger at you, judge you according to your behavior, and repay you for all your detestable practices.

Ezekiel 7:9 I won't be showing pity or compassion. I'll repay you according to your behavior while your detestable practices remain among you. And you'll know that I, the LORD, have been attacking you.

Ezekiel 7:27 "The king will mourn, the prince will be clothed with desolation, and the hands of the people of the land will tremble. I'll deal with them according to their behavior and I will judge them by how they've judged. Then they'll learn that I am the LORD."

Ezekiel 11:21 But to those whose hearts delight in loathsome things and detestable practices, I'll bring the consequences of their behavior crashing down on their own heads," declares the Lord GOD.'"

Ezekiel 13:22 "Because you've dismayed the heart of the righteous—whom I never intended to dismay—with lies, and because you've encouraged the wicked so that he wouldn't abandon his evil behavior and by doing so live,

Ezekiel 16:43 Because you didn't remember the time when you were young, but instead you provoked me to anger because of all these things, watch out! I'm going to bring your behavior back to haunt you!" declares the Lord GOD. "Didn't you do this wicked thing, in addition to all your other detestable practices?"

Ezekiel 16:47 It wasn't just that you lived like they did and committed their detestable practices, but in just a little while your behavior led you to become more corrupt than they were!"

Ezekiel 16:61 Then you'll remember your behavior and be ashamed when you greet your sisters—your elder sister and your younger sister. I'll give them to you as daughters, but not on account of my covenant with you.

Ezekiel 18:25 "Yet you keep saying, 'The LORD isn't being consistent with his standards.' Pay attention, you house of Israel: Is my behavior really inconsistent with my standards? Isn't it your behavior that isn't just?

Ezekiel 18:27 When a wicked person quits his wicked behavior and does what's just and right, he'll be enabled to live.

Ezekiel 18:30 "Therefore, Israel, I'm going to judge you according to the behavior of each and every one of you," declares the Lord GOD. "So repent and turn from all your sins so that sin won't keep on being a stumbling block for you.

Ezekiel 22:31 so I poured my indignation over them. With my fierce anger, I've consumed them. I brought the consequences of their behavior upon them,' declares the Lord GOD."

Ezekiel 28:15 You were blameless in your behavior from the day you were created until wickedness was discovered in you.

Ezekiel 33:8 If I should say to a certain wicked person, "You wicked Man, you're certainly about to die," but you don't warn him to turn from his wicked behavior, he'll die in his guilt, but I'll seek retribution for his bloodshed from you.

Ezekiel 33:9 However, if you warn the wicked to turn from his behavior and he does not do so, he will die in his guilt, and you will have saved yourself.'"

Hosea 4:9 So it will be: like people, like priest. I will punish them for their lifestyles, rewarding them according to their behavior.

Micah 7:13 The land will become desolate because of its inhabitants, and as a result of their behavior.

Galatians 2:13 The other Jews also joined him in this hypocritical behavior, to the extent that even Barnabas was caught up in their hypocrisy.

1 Timothy 4:12 Do not let anyone look down on you because you are young, but be an example for other believers in your speech, behavior, love, faithfulness, and purity.

Malachi 3:3 He will sit refining and purifying silver, purifying the descendants of Levi, refining them like gold and silver. Then they'll bring a righteous offering to the LORD.

1 Peter 1:6 You greatly rejoice in this, even though you have to suffer various kinds of trial for a little while, ⁷so that your genuine faith, which is more valuable than gold that perishes when tested by fire, may result in praise, glory, and honor when Jesus, the Messiah, is revealed.

Exodus 1:7 But the Israelis were fruitful and increased abundantly. They multiplied in numbers and became very, very strong. As a result, the land was filled with them.

Numbers 13:18 See what the land is like. Observe whether the people who live there are strong or weak, or whether they're few or numerous.

Numbers 13:28 except that the people who have settled in the land are strong, and their cities are greatly fortified. We also saw the descendants of Anak.

Numbers 13:31 "We can't attack those people," the Men who were with him said, "because they're too strong compared to us."

Numbers 21:24 But Israel defeated him in battle and took possession of all his lands from Arnon to Jabbok, including the Ammonites, even though the border of the Ammonites was strong.

Deuteronomy 2:36 From Aroer on the edge of Arnon Valley and from the town all the way to Gilead, there was no city that was too strong for us—the LORD our God delivered them all to us.

Deuteronomy 3:28 Therefore charge Joshua to be doubly strong, for he will lead this people and cause them to inherit the land that you'll see.'

Deuteronomy 9:2 The Anakim are strong and tall, and you know them. You've heard it said, 'Who can stand up against the Anakim?'

Deuteronomy 11:8 "Keep all the commands that I'm giving you today, so you can be strong enough to enter and possess the land that you are crossing over to inherit

Deuteronomy 14:26 You may spend the money to your heart's content to buy livestock, flocks, wine, strong drink, and whatever you desire. You and your household may eat there and rejoice in the presence of the LORD your God."

Deuteronomy 31:6 Be strong and courageous. Don't fear or tremble before them, because the LORD your God will be the One who keeps on walking with you—he won't leave you or abandon you."

Deuteronomy 31:7 Then Moses called on Joshua and told him in the presence of everyone in Israel, "Be strong and courageous, because you'll bring this people to the land that the LORD your God had promised to give your ancestors. You will be the one who causes them to possess it.

Deuteronomy 31:23 Then the LORD charged Nun's son Joshua, "Be strong and courageous, because you'll bring the Israelis to the land that I promised to them by an oath. I'll be with you."

Deuteronomy 34:7 Moses was 120 years old when he died. His eyesight wasn't impaired and he was still vigorous and strong.

Joshua 1:6 "Be strong and courageous, because you'll be leading this people to inherit the land that I promised to give their ancestors.

Joshua 1:7 Only be strong and very courageous to ensure that you obey all the instructions that my servant Moses gave you—turn neither to the right nor to the left from it—so that you may succeed wherever you go.

Joshua 1:9 "I've commanded you, haven't I? Be strong and courageous. Don't be fearful or discouraged, because the LORD your God is with you wherever you go."

Joshua 1:18 Anyone who rebels against what you say and doesn't listen to your words regarding everything that you command will be executed. Only be strong and courageous."

Joshua 4:24 Do this so that all of the people of the earth may know how strong the power of the LORD is, and so that you may fear the LORD your God every day."

Joshua 10:25 Joshua told the army, "Don't fear or be dismayed! Be strong and courageous, because this is how the LORD will treat all of your enemies whom you fight."

Joshua 14:11 I'm still as strong today as I was the day Moses commissioned me. I'm as strong today as I was then, and I can go out to battle and come back successful.

Joshua 17:13 Later on, when the Israelis had become strong, they forced the Canaanites to work for them, but they never did expel them completely.

Joshua 17:18 but the hill country will also belong to you. Even though it's a forest, you will clear it and possess it to its farthest borders. You'll drive out the Canaanites, even though they have iron chariots and even though they're strong."

Joshua 23:6 "Stand very strong, then, so you can obey and carry out everything written in the Book of the Law of Moses, turning neither to the right nor to the left of it.

Joshua 23:9 because the LORD has expelled great and strong nations ahead of you. Now as for you, not a single Man has been able to oppose you right to this day.

Judges 1:28 When Israel had grown strong, they subjected the Canaanites to conscripted labor and never did expel them completely.

Judges 1:35 Furthermore, the Amorites continued to inhabit Mount Heres in Aijalon and Shaalbim. Eventually, however, after the tribe of Joseph had become strong, the Amorites were subjected to conscripted labor.

Judges 3:10 The Spirit of the LORD was on him, and he governed Israel. When Othniel went out to battle, the LORD handed king Cushan-rishathaim of Aram-naharaim into his control, and Othniel's domination of Cushan-rishathaim was strong.

Judges 3:29 At that time they attacked about 10,000 Moabites, all of whom were strong and valiant Men. Not one Man escaped.

Judges 13:24 Later on, the Woman gave birth to a son and named him Samson. The child grew strong and the LORD blessed him.

Judges 18:26 Then the descendants of Dan went on their way. Because Micah saw that they were too strong for him, he turned and went back home.

1 Samuel 4:9 Philistines, be strong and be Men, or you will become slaves to the Hebrews just as they have been slaves to you! Be Men and fight!"

1 Samuel 14:52 There was intense fighting against the Philistines during Saul's entire reign, and whenever Saul discovered a strong or valiant warrior, he would enlist him for service.

1 Samuel 23:13 David and his Men, about 600 strong, got up and left Keilah. They moved around wherever they could go. Saul was advised that David had escaped from Keilah, so he stopped the campaign.

2 Samuel 3:1 After this, a state of protracted war existed between Saul's dynasty and David's dynasty, and the dynasty of David continued to grow and become strong while the dynasty of Saul continued to grow weaker.

2 Samuel 10:12 Be strong, be courageous on behalf of our people and for the cities of our God, and may the LORD do what he thinks is best."

2 Samuel 17:8 "You know how strong your father and his Men are. They're as mad as a bear robbed of her cubs! Furthermore, your father is a skilled warrior. He won't stay with his army at night.

1 Kings 2:2 "I'm headed down the road that everyone who lives on earth travels, so be strong and demonstrate that you're a grown Man

1 Chronicles 11:10 These are the leaders of the elite warriors who were strong supporters of David in his kingdom, along with all of Israel, in keeping with the message from the LORD concerning Israel.

1 Corinthians 19:13 Be strong, be courageous on behalf of our people and for the cities of our God, and may the LORD do what he thinks is best."

1 Corinthians 22:13 Then you will be successful, if you keep on observing the statutes and ordinances that the LORD commanded Moses concerning Israel. Be strong, be courageous, and never give in to fear or dismay.

1 Corinthians 28:10 So keep watching, because the LORD has chosen you to build the Temple of his sanctuary. So be strong, and get to work!"

1 Corinthians 28:20 David continued with these words for his son Solomon: "Be strong and courageous, and get to work. Never be afraid or discouraged, for the LORD God, my God, is with you. He will not fail you nor will he abandon you right up to your completion of the work for the service of the Temple of the LORD.

1 Corinthians 29:12 Both wealth and honor proceed from you, and you are ruling over them all. You control power—you control who is made great, and how everyone becomes strong.

2 Chronicles 15:7 Now as for you, be strong and never be discouraged, because there will be reward for your work."

2 Chronicles 22:9 Jehu also searched for Ahaziah, had him apprehended while Ahaziah was hiding out in Samaria, and had Ahaziah brought to him. Jehu had Ahaziah executed and buried. It was said of Jehu, "He is the son of Jehoshaphat, who sought the LORD with all of his heart." As a result, there was no one left in the household of Ahaziah strong enough to reign in the kingdom.

2 Chronicles 26:15 He also had various siege engines built by skilled designers and placed them on the towers and on the corner ramparts that could fire arrows and very large stones. His reputation spread far and wide, and he was marvelously assisted until he grew very strong.

2 Chronicles 26:16 But after he had become strong, in his arrogance he acted corruptly and became unfaithful to the LORD his God, and he dared to enter the LORD's Temple to burn incense on the incense altar.

2 Chronicles 32:7 "Be strong and courageous. Don't be afraid or disheartened because of the king of Assyria or because of the army that accompanies him, because the one who is with us is greater than the one with him.

Ezra 9:12 So, therefore, do not give your daughters in marriage to their sons, nor marry their daughters to your sons, and under no circumstances are you to seek their well-being or their wealth, so that you may remain strong, enjoying the best things the land has to give, and so that you may establish an inheritance for your children forever.'

Ezra 10:4 So get up—it's your responsibility! We're with you. Be strong, and get to work."

Nehemiah 1:10 These are your servants as well as your people, whom you have redeemed by your great power and by your strong hand.

Job 6:12 Am I as strong as a rock? Am I some kind of iron Man?

Job 9:4 He is wise in heart and strong in will—who can be stubborn against him and succeed?

Job 18:7 His strong steps are restricted, and his own advice trips him up.

Job 24:22 God prolongs the life of the strong by his power, but they get up in the morning without purpose in life.

Job 36:5 "Indeed God is mighty and he doesn't show disrespect; he is mighty and strong of heart.

Job 39:4 Their young are strong; they grow up in the open field; then they go off and don't return to them."

Job 40:18 His bones are conduits of bronze; his strong bones are like bars of iron.

Job 41:24 His heart is as strong as stone, it is as hard as a lower millstone.

Psalms 18:17 He delivered me from my strong enemies, from those who hated me because they were stronger than I.

Psalms 21:13 Rise up, LORD, because you are strong; we will sing and praise your power.

Psalms 24:8 Who is the King of Glory? The LORD strong and mighty, the LORD, mighty in battle.

Psalms 30:7 By your favor, LORD, you established me as a strong mountain; Then you hid your face, and I was dismayed.

Psalms 31:24 Be strong, and let your heart be courageous, all you who put your hope in the LORD.

Psalms 40:4 How blessed is that strong person who places his trust in the LORD, and who has not acknowledged the proud nor resorted to lies.

Psalms 45:4 In your majesty ride forth for the cause of truth, humility, and righteousness; and your strong right hand will teach you awesome things.

Psalms 62:7 I rely on God who is my deliverance and my glory; he is my strong rock, and my refuge is in God.

Psalms 71:7 I have become an example to many that you are my strong refuge.

Psalms 89:13 Your arm is strong; your hand is mighty; indeed, your right hand is victorious.

Psalms 136:12 with a strong hand and an active arm, for his gracious love is everlasting.

Psalms 140:7 LORD, my Lord, my strong deliverer, you have protected my head in the time of battle.

Psalms 142:6 Pay attention to my cry, for I have been brought very low. Deliver me from my tormentors, for they are far too strong for me.

Psalms 144:2 he is my gracious love and my fortress, my strong tower and my deliverer, my shield and the one in whom I find refuge, who subdues peoples under me.

Proverbs 4:3 When I was a son to my father, not yet strong and an only son to my mother,

Proverbs 6:34 because jealousy incites a strong Man's rage, and he will show no mercy when it's time for revenge.

Proverbs 18:10 The name of the LORD is a strong tower; a righteous person rushes to it and is lifted up above the danger.

Proverbs 18:18 Casting dice settles a dispute, deciding between strong contenders.

Proverbs 23:11 for strong is their Redeemer who will take up their case against you.

Proverbs 24:5 A wise Man is strong, and a knowledgeable Man grows in strength.

Ecclesiastes 9:11 I considered and observed on earth the following: The race doesn't go to the swift, nor the battle to the strong, nor food to the wise, nor wealth to the smart, nor recognition to the skilled. Instead, timing and circumstances meet them all.

Ecclesiastes 12:3 when that day comes, the palace guards will tremble, strong Men will stoop down, Women grinders will cease because they are few, and the sight of those who peer through the lattice will grow dim.

Song of Solomon 8:6 Set me like a seal over your heart, like a seal on your arm. For love is as strong as death, passion as intense as Sheol. The flames of love are flames of fire, a blaze that comes from the LORD.

Isaiah 5:22 "How terrible it will be for those who are heroes at drinking wine, and champions in mixing strong drink,

Isaiah 17:4 "At that time, Jacob's glory will have become weakened, and his strong flesh will turn gaunt;

Isaiah 25:3 Therefore strong peoples will glorify you; cities of ruthless nations will revere you.

Isaiah 26:1 At that time, people will sing this song in the land of Judah: "We have a strong city; God crafts victory, its walls and ramparts.

Isaiah 28:2 Look! The LORD has one who is mighty and strong, like a hailstorm and destructive tempest, like a storm of mighty, overflowing water—and he will give rest to the land.

Isaiah 28:7 These people also stagger from wine and reel from strong drink. Priests and prophets stagger from strong drink; they're drunk from wine; they reel from strong drink, waver when seeing visions, and stumble when rendering decisions.

Isaiah 29:9 "Act stupid! Be astonished! Act blind, and be blind! Be drunk, but not from wine; stagger around, but not from strong drink.

Isaiah 31:1 "How terrible it will be for those who go down to Egypt for help, who rely on horses, who trust in the chariot, because there are so many, and in charioteers, because they are so strong—but do not look to the Holy One of Israel or seek the LORD!

Isaiah 35:4 Say to those with anxious hearts, 'Be strong, do not be afraid! Here is your God—he will bring vengeance, he will bring divine retribution, and he will save you.'

Isaiah 41:6 Each helps his neighbor, saying to each other, 'Be strong!'

Isaiah 53:12 Therefore I will allot him a portion with the great, and he will divide the spoils with the strong; because he poured out his life to death, and was numbered with the transgressors; yet he carried the sins of many, and made intercession for their transgressions."

Jeremiah 9:23 This is what the LORD says: "The wise Man is not to boast in his wisdom; the strong Man is not to boast in his strength; and the rich Man is not to boast in his riches.

Jeremiah 14:9 Why are you like a Man taken by surprise, like a strong Man who can't deliver? You are among us, LORD, and your name is the one by which we're called. Don't abandon us!

Jeremiah 21:5 Because of my anger, wrath, and great fury, I'll fight against you myself with an outstretched hand and a strong arm.

Jeremiah 32:21 By your strong hand and outstretched arm, and with great terror, you brought your people Israel out of the land of Egypt with signs and wonders.

Jeremiah 48:14 "How can you say, 'We're strong warriors, and soldiers ready for battle'?

Ezekiel 2:4 They're stubborn and strong willed. I'm sending you to them to tell them what the LORD says.

Ezekiel 22:14 Can your heart stand up to this? Can your hands remain strong when I deal with you? I, the LORD, have spoken and will fulfill this.

Daniel 2:42 Just as their toes and feet are part iron and part clay, so will the kingdom be both strong and brittle.

Daniel 4:22 it's you, your majesty! You've become great and strong, your greatness has grown to the heavens, and your dominion reaches to the distant parts of the earth.

Daniel 10:19 and said, 'Don't be afraid, Man highly regarded. Be at peace, and be strong.' "As soon as he spoke to me, I gained strength and replied, 'Sir, please speak, now that you've strengthened me.'

Daniel 11:5 ""The southern king will become strong, along with one of his officials, who will become stronger than he and rule over his own realm with great power.

Daniel 11:32 Through flattery he'll corrupt those who act wickedly toward the covenant, but people who know their God will be strong and take action.

Joel 1:6 Indeed, a nation has invaded my land—it is strong and its population is too large to count—with teeth like a lion and fangs like a lioness.

Joel 2:2 A day of doom and gloom, a day of clouds and shadows like the dawn spreads out to cover the mountains—a people strong and robust. Never has there been anything like it, neither will anything follow to compare with it, even through the lifetime of generation upon generation."

Nahum 3:14 Draw water, because a siege is coming! Strengthen your fortresses! Make the clay good and strong! Mix the mortar! Go get your brick molds!

Haggai 2:4 Now be strong, Zerubbabel,' declares the LORD, 'and be strong, Joshua son of Jehozadak, the high priest, and be strong, all you people of the land,' declares the LORD. 'Go to work, because I am with you,' declares the LORD of the Heavenly Armies.

Zechariah 8:9 "This is what the LORD of the Heavenly Armies says: 'Be strong so the Temple can be built, you who are now listening to this message spoken by the prophets when the foundation was laid to the Temple of the LORD of the Heavenly Armies.

Matthew 12:29 How can someone go into a strong Man's house and carry off his possessions without first tying up the strong Man? Then he can ransack his house.

Luke 1:15 because he will be great in the Lord's presence. He will never drink wine or any strong drink, and he will be filled with the Holy Spirit even before he is born.

Luke 1:80 Now the child continued to grow and to become spiritually strong. He lived in the wilderness until the day he appeared in Israel.

Luke 11:21 "When a strong Man, fully armed, guards his own Mansion, his property is safe.

Romans 1:11 For I am longing to see you so that I may impart to you some spiritual gift to make you strong,

Romans 15:1 Now we who are strong ought to be patient with the weaknesses of those who are not strong and must stop pleasing ourselves.

1 Corinthians 1:8 He will keep you strong until the end, so that you will be blameless on the Day of our Lord Jesus the Messiah.

1 Corinthians 4:10 We are fools for the Messiah's sake, but you are wise in the Messiah. We are weak, but you are strong. You are honored, but we are dishonored.

1 Corinthians 16:13 Remain alert. Keep standing firm in your faith. Keep on being courageous and strong.

2 Corinthians12:10 That is why I take such pleasure in weaknesses, insults, hardships, persecutions, and difficulties for the Messiah's sake, for when I am weak, then I am strong.

2 Corinthians 13:9 We are glad when we are weak and you are strong. That is what we are praying for—your maturity.

Ephesians 6:10 Finally, be strong in the Lord, relying on his mighty strength.

1 Thessalonians 2:2 As you know, we suffered persecution and were mistreated in Philippi. Yet we were encouraged by our God to tell you his gospel in spite of strong opposition.

1 Thessalonians 3:13 Then your hearts will be strong, blameless, and holy in the presence of God, who is our Father, when our Lord Jesus appears with all his saints.

1 Timothy 4:16 Pay close attention to your life and your teaching. Persevere in these things, because if you do so, you will save both yourself and those who listen to you.

2 Timothy 2:1 As for you, my child, be strong by the grace that is in the Messiah Jesus.

James 3:4 And look at ships! They are so big that it takes strong winds to drive them, yet they are steered by a tiny rudder wherever the helmsman directs.

1 John 2:14 I have written to you, little children, because you have known the Father. I have written to you, fathers, because you have known the one who has existed from the beginning. I have written to you, young people, because you are strong and because God's word remains in you and you have overcome the evil one.

1 John 3:19 This is how we will know that we belong to the truth and how we will be able to keep ourselves strong in his presence.

Chapter IV.

A Warrior Is Wise.

Genesis 41:33 Therefore let Pharaoh select a wise, discerning person to place in charge over the land of Egypt.

Genesis 41:39 "Since God has revealed all of this to you," Pharaoh told Joseph, "there is no one so wise and discerning as you.

Deuteronomy 1:13 Choose for yourselves wise and discerning Men, known to your tribes, and appoint them as your leaders.

Deuteronomy 1:15 So I chose leaders from your tribes, wise and respected Men, and I appointed them over you—comManders of thousands, hundreds, fifties, and tens.

Deuteronomy 4:6 Observe them carefully, for this will show your wisdom and discernment in the eyes of people who'll listen to all these decrees. Then they'll say: 'Surely this great nation is a wise and discerning people.'

Deuteronomy 16:19 You must not twist justice, show favoritism, or take bribes, because a bribe blinds the eyes of the wise and subverts the speech of the righteous.

Deuteronomy 29:9 Therefore, keep the terms of this covenant, carrying them out so that you'll be wise in everything you do."

Deuteronomy 32:29 O, that they were wise to understand this and consider their future!

1 Samuel 12:15 But if you don't obey the LORD and rebel against the commandment of the LORD, then the LORD will turn against you as he did against your ancestors.

2 Samuel 14:20 intending to change the outcome of this matter. Nevertheless, your majesty is wise, like the wisdom of the angel of God, to be aware of everything that's going on throughout the earth."

1 Kings 2:9 But don't let him off unpunished, since you're a wise Man and you'll know what you need to do to him. Find a way that he dies in his old age by shedding his blood."

1 Kings 3:12 look how I'm going to do precisely what you asked. I'm giving you a wise and discerning mind, so that there will have been no one like you before you and no one will arise after you like you.

1 Kings 5:7 As soon as Hiram received the message from Solomon, he became so ecstatic that he exclaimed, "Blessed be the LORD today, who has given David a wise son to rule this great people!" Then he sent this message to Solomon:

1 Kings 7:14 the son of a widow from the tribe of Naphtali, whose father was from Tyre. A bronze worker, he was wise, knowledgeable, and was skilled in all sorts of bronze working. He went to King Solomon and did all of his work.

1 Kings 10:24 All the earth continued to seek audiences with Solomon so they could hear the wise things that God had put in his heart.

2 Chronicles 9:23 All the kings of the earth continued to seek audiences with Solomon so they could hear the wise things that God had put in his heart.

2 Chronicles 11:23 Rehoboam was wise to distribute some his children throughout all of the territories of Judah and Benjamin, placing them in all of the fortified cities. He allotted them abundant supplies of food and sought many wives for them.

Esther 1:13 The king spoke to the wise Men who understood the times, for it was the king's custom to consult all those who understood law and justice.

Job 9:4 He is wise in heart and strong in will—who can be stubborn against him and succeed?

Job 12:13 With God is wisdom and strength; counsel and understanding belongs to him.

Job 13:5 I wish you'd all just shut up. Then at least you would appear to be wise.

Job 22:2 "Can a human being be useful to God, since he, who is wise, is sufficient to himself?

Job 32:9 "The aged aren't always wise, nor do the elderly always understand justice.

Job 34:2 "Listen to what I have to say, you wise Men! Pay attention to me, you educated people!

Job 34:34 "Men of understanding, speak to me! Are any of you Men wise? Then listen to me!

Job 37:24 Therefore humanity fears him, which none of the wise can quite comprehend."

Psalms 48:14 For this God is our God forever and ever; he will be our guide even to the end.

Psalms 19:7 The Law of the LORD is perfect, restoring life. The testimony of the LORD is steadfast, making foolish people wise.

Psalms 73:24 You will guide me with your wise advice, and later you will receive me with honor.

Psalms 94:8 Pay attention, you dull ones among the crowds! You fools! Will you ever become wise?

Psalms 105:22 to discipline his rulers at will and make his elders wise.

Psalms 107:43 Let whoever is wise observe these things, that they may comprehend the gracious love of the LORD.

Proverbs 1:3 for acquiring the discipline that produces wise behavior, righteousness, justice, and upright living;

Proverbs 1:5 Let the wise listen and increase their learning; let the person of understanding receive guidance

Proverbs 3:7 Do not be wise in your own opinion. Fear the LORD and turn away from evil.

Proverbs 3:35 The wise will inherit honor, but he holds fools up for ridicule.

Proverbs 8:33 Listen to instruction and be wise. Don't ignore it.

Proverbs 9:8 Don't rebuke a mocker or he will hate you. Rebuke a wise person, and he will love you.

Proverbs 9:9 Counsel a wise Man, and he will be wiser still; teach a righteous Man, and he will add to his learning.

Proverbs 9:12 If you are wise, your wisdom will assist you. If you mock, you alone will be held responsible.

Proverbs 10:1 The proverbs of Solomon. A wise son brings joy to his father, but a foolish son grieves his mother.

Proverbs 10:8 The wise person accepts commands, but the chattering fool will be brought down.

Proverbs 10:14 Those who are wise store up knowledge, but when the fool speaks, destruction is near.

Proverbs 11:29 Whoever troubles his household will inherit the wind, and the fool will be a servant to the wise.

Proverbs 11:30 The fruit of the righteous is a tree of life, and the one who wins people is wise.

Proverbs 12:8 A Man is praised because of his wise words, but the perverted mind will be despised.

Proverbs 12:15 The lifestyle of the fool is right in his own opinion, but wise is the Man who listens to advice.

Proverbs 12:18 Some speak rashly like the cutting of a sword, but what the wise say promotes healing.

Proverbs 13:1 A wise son heeds a father's correction, but a mocker does not listen to rebuke.

Proverbs 13:10 Arrogance only brings quarreling, but those receiving advice are wise.

Proverbs 13:14 What the wise have to teach is a fountain of life and causes someone to avoid the snares of death.

Proverbs 13:20 Whoever keeps company with the wise becomes wise, but the companion of fools suffers harm.

Proverbs 14:3 What a fool says brings a rod to his back, but the words of the wise protect them.

Proverbs 14:16 The wise person fears and turns away from evil, but a fool is reckless and overconfident.

Proverbs 14:24 The crown of the wise is their wealth, but the stupidity of fools is just that—stupidity!

Proverbs 14:35 The king approves the wise servant, but he is angry at anyone who acts shamefully.

Proverbs 15:2 The wise speak, presenting knowledge appropriately, but fools spout foolishness.

Proverbs 15:7 What the wise have to say disseminates knowledge, but it's not in the heart of fools to do so.

Proverbs 15:12 The arrogant mocker never loves the one who corrects him; he will not inquire of the wise.

Proverbs 15:24 The way of life leads upward for the wise so he may avoid Sheol below.

Proverbs 15:31 Whoever listens to a life-giving rebuke will be at home among the wise.

Proverbs 16:14 The king's wrath results in a death sentence, but whoever is wise will appease him.

Proverbs 16:21 The wise-hearted person is told to be discerning, and pleasant speech promotes instruction.

Proverbs 16:23 A wise person's thoughts control his words, and his speech promotes instruction.

Proverbs 17:28 Even a fool is thought to be wise when he remains silent; he is thought to be prudent when he keeps his mouth shut.

Proverbs 18:15 The mind of a discerning person gains knowledge, while the ears of wise people seek out knowledge.

Proverbs 19:20 Listen to advice and accept discipline, and you'll be wise for the rest of your life.

Proverbs 20:26 A wise king sifts the wicked, crushing them with the threshing wheel.

Proverbs 21:11 When a mocker is punished, the fool gains wisdom; but when the wise is instructed, he receives knowledge.

Proverbs 21:20 Precious treasures and oil are found where the wise live, but a foolish Man devours them.

Proverbs 21:22 A wise Man attacks the city of the mighty, bringing down the fortress in which they trust.

Proverbs 22:17 Pay attention and listen to the words of the wise, and apply your heart to my teaching,

Proverbs 23:9 Don't speak when a fool is listening, because he'll despise your wise words.

Proverbs 23:15 My son, if your heart is wise, my own heart will greatly rejoice.

Proverbs 23:19 Listen, my son, and be wise, commit yourself to live God's way.

Proverbs 23:24 The father of a righteous person will greatly rejoice; whoever fathers a wise son will be glad because of him.

Proverbs 24:5 A wise Man is strong, and a knowledgeable Man grows in strength.

Proverbs 24:6 For through wise counsel you will wage your war, and victory lies in an abundance of advisors.

Proverbs 25:12 Like a gold earring and a necklace of pure gold is a wise reprover to a listening ear.

Proverbs 26:5 Answer a fool according to his foolishness, or he will think himself to be wise.

Proverbs 26:12 Do you see a Man who is wise in his own opinion? There's more hope for a fool than for him.

Proverbs 27:11 Be wise, my son, and make me happy, so I can reply to anyone who insults me.

Proverbs 28:11 The rich Man may be wise in his own opinion; but a discerning, poor Man sees through him.

Proverbs 29:8 Scornful Men enflame a city, but the wise defuse anger.

Proverbs 29:9 When a wise Man has a dispute with a fool, the fool either rages or laughs without relief.

Proverbs 29:11 The fool vents all his feelings, but the wise person keeps them to himself.

Proverbs 2:9 So I became great, greater than anyone who had lived before me in Jerusalem. Throughout all of this, I remained wise.

Ecclesiastes 2:14 The wise use their eyes, but the fool walks in darkness. I also perceived that the same outcome affects them all.

Ecclesiastes 4:13 A poor but wise youth is better than an old but foolish king who will no longer accept correction.

Ecclesiastes 7:4 For the wise person thinks carefully when in mourning, but fools focus their thoughts on pleasure.

Ecclesiastes 7:5 It is better to listen to a wise person's rebuke than to listen to the praise of fools.

Ecclesiastes 7:11 Wise use of possessions is good; it brings benefit to the living.

Ecclesiastes 7:19 Wisdom given as strength to a wise person is better than having ten powerful Men in the city.

Ecclesiastes 7:28 Among the things I seek but have not found: one Man among a thousand I did find, but I have not found one Woman to be wise among all these.

Ecclesiastes 8:1 Who is really wise? Who knows how to interpret this saying: "A person's wisdom improves his appearance, softening a harsh countenance."

Ecclesiastes 8:5 Whoever obeys his commands will not experience harm, and the wise in heart will discern both the appropriate time and response.

Ecclesiastes 9:17 The softly spoken words of the wise are to be heard rather than the shouts of a ruler of fools.

Ecclesiastes 10:12 The words spoken by the wise are gracious, but the lips of a fool will devour him.

Ecclesiastes 12:9 Moreover, besides being wise himself, the Teacher taught people what he had learned by listening, making inquiries, and composing many proverbs.

Ecclesiastes 12:11 Sayings from the wise are like cattle prods and well fastened nails; this masterful collection was given by one shepherd.

Isaiah 19:12 Where are your wise Men now? Let them tell you, let them make known what the LORD has planned against Egypt.

Jeremiah 51:57 I'll make their leaders, their wise Men, their governors, their deputies, and their warriors drunk so that they sleep forever and don't wake up," declares the King whose name is the LORD of the Heavenly Armies.

Daniel 2:21 It is God who alters the times and seasons, and he removes kings and promotes kings. He gives wisdom to the wise and knowledge to the discerning.

Hosea 14:9 Whoever is wise, let him understand these things. Whoever is discerning, let him know them. For the ways of the LORD are right: the righteous follow his example, but the rebellious stumble in them.

Matthew 23:34 "That is why I am sending you prophets, wise Men, and scribes. Some of them you will kill and crucify, and some of them you will whip in your synagogues and persecute from town to town.

Matthew 24:45 "Who, then, is the faithful and wise servant whom his master has put in charge of his household to give the others their food at the right time?

Matthew 25:2 Now five of them were foolish, and five were wise,

Matthew 25:4 But the wise ones took flasks of oil with their lamps.

Matthew 25:8 But the foolish ones told the wise, 'Give us some of your oil, because our lamps are going out!'

Matthew 25:9 But the wise ones replied, 'No! There will never be enough for us and for you. You'd better go to the dealers and buy some for yourselves.'

Romans 16:19 For your obedience has become known to everyone, and I am full of joy for you. But I want you to be wise about what is good, and innocent about what is evil.

1 Corinthians 1:20 Where is the wise person? Where is the scholar? Where is the philosopher of this age? God has turned the wisdom of the world into nonsense, hasn't he?

1 Corinthians 6:5 I say this to make you feel ashamed. Has it come to this, that there is not one person among you who is wise enough to settle disagreements between brothers?

2 Corinthians 11:19 You are wise, so you will gladly be tolerant of fools.

Ephesians 1:17 I pray that the God of our Lord Jesus, the Messiah, the most glorious Father, would give you a wise spirit, along with revelation that comes through knowing the Messiah fully.

Ephesians 5:15 So, then, be careful how you live. Do not be unwise but wise.

James 1:19 You must understand this, my dear brothers. Everyone should be quick to listen, slow to speak, and slow to get angry.

James 3:13 Who among you is wise and understanding? Let him show by his noble conduct that his actions are done humbly and wisely.

Chapter V.

A Warrior Serves God Above All Else.

Exodus 10:8 Moses and Aaron were brought back to Pharaoh and he told them, "Go, serve the LORD your God. But exactly who will go?"

Exodus 10:26 And even our livestock must go with us. Not a hoof will be left behind because we will use some of them to serve the LORD our God, and until we get there we won't know what we need to serve the LORD."

Exodus 20:5 You are not to bow down to them in worship or serve them; because I, the LORD your God, am a jealous God, punishing the children for the iniquity of the parents, to the third and fourth generations of those who hate me,

Exodus 23:25 You are to serve the LORD your God, and he will bless your food and water, and I'll remove sickness from you.

Deuteronomy 6:13 Fear the LORD your God, serve him, and make your oaths in his name.

Deuteronomy 7:16 You are to utterly destroy everyone whom the LORD your God will deliver to you. Do not have pity on them nor serve their gods. Otherwise, they will become a snare for you."

Deuteronomy 8:19 If you neglect the LORD your God, follow other gods, and serve and worship them, I testify to you today that you will certainly be destroyed.

Deuteronomy 10:12 "Now Israel, what does the LORD your God desire from you? Only this: fear him, walk in all his ways, love him, serve him with all your heart and in all your life,

Deuteronomy 10:20 You are to fear the LORD your God and serve him. Cling to him and swear by his name.

Deuteronomy 11:13 "If you carefully observe the commands that I'm giving you today, to love the LORD your God and serve him with all your heart and soul,

Deuteronomy 13:4 You must follow the LORD your God, fear him, observe his commandments, listen to his voice, serve him, and cling to him.

Deuteronomy 18:5 For the LORD your God has chosen them and their descendants from among your tribes to stand and serve in the name of the LORD all their lives."

Deuteronomy 28:47 "Because you didn't serve the LORD your God joyfully and wholeheartedly, despite the abundance of everything you have,

Deuteronomy 28:48 you'll serve your enemies whom the LORD your God will send against you. You will serve in famine and in drought, in nakedness, and in lack of everything. They'll set a yoke of iron upon your neck until they have exterminated you.

Deuteronomy 29:18 Be alert so there is no Man, Woman, family, or a tribe whose heart is turning away from the LORD your God to go and serve the gods of those nations. "Be alert so there will be no root among you that produces poisonous and bitter fruit,

Joshua 22:5 Only be very careful to keep the commands and the Law that Moses the servant of the LORD commanded you—that is, to love the LORD your God, to follow in all of his ways, to keep his commands, to stay close to him, and to serve him with all your heart and soul."

Joshua 23:16 When you break the covenant of the LORD your God that he commanded you to obey by going to serve other gods and worship them, then the anger of the LORD will blaze against you, and you will perish quickly from this good land that he gave you."

Joshua 24:18 The LORD expelled all the people before us, including the Amorites who lived in the land. Therefore, we also will serve the LORD, for he is our God."

Joshua 24:24 The people replied, "We will serve the LORD our God and obey his voice."

Judges 10:10 Then the Israelis cried out to the LORD and told him, "We have sinned against you because we have abandoned our God to serve the Baals."

1 Samuel 12:14 If you fear the LORD, serve him, obey him, and don't rebel against the commandment of the LORD, then both you and the king who rules over you will truly follow the LORD your God.

1 Chronicles 28:9 "Now as for you, my son Solomon, get to know the God of your father. Serve him with a sound heart and a devoted soul, because the LORD is searching every heart, every plan and thought. He will be found by you, assuming you are seeking him, but if you abandon him, he will abandon you forever.

2 Chronicles 30:8 So don't be stiff-necked like your ancestors were. Instead, submit to the LORD, enter his sanctuary that he has sanctified forever, and serve the LORD your God so that he'll stop being angry with you.

2 Chronicles 34:33 Josiah also removed all the detestable things from the territories that belonged to the people of Israel, and made everyone who lived in Israel to serve the LORD their God. For the rest of his life, they didn't abandon their quest to follow the LORD God of their ancestors.

Jeremiah 5:19 When the people ask, 'Why has the LORD our God done all this to us?' you are to say to them, 'Just as you have forsaken me and served foreign gods in your land, so you will serve strangers in a land that is not yours.'"

Ezekiel 20:20 You are to make my Sabbaths holy, and you are to let them serve as a sign between you and me, so that you may know that I am the LORD your God."

Ezekiel 20:39 "And now, you house of Israel, this is what the Lord GOD says, 'Go ahead and serve your idols, both now and later, but later you'll listen to me, and you won't profane my sacred name again by your offerings and idols.

Daniel 6:16 At this point, the king ordered Daniel brought in and thrown into the lions' pit. The king spoke to Daniel, "Your God, whom you serve constantly, will deliver you himself."

Daniel 6:20 As he approached where Daniel was in the pit, he cried out to him in a voice filled with anguish, "Daniel, servant of the living God, has your God, whom you serve constantly, been able to deliver you from the lions?"

Matthew 4:10 Then Jesus told him, "Go away, Satan! Because it is written, 'You must worship the Lord your God and serve only him.'"

Matthew 6:24 "No one can serve two masters, because either he will hate one and love the other, or be loyal to one and despise the other. You cannot serve God and riches!"

Matthew 6:33 But first be concerned about God's kingdom and his righteousness, and all of these things will be provided for you as well.

Luke 4:8 But Jesus answered him, "It is written, 'You must worship the Lord your God and serve only him.'"

Acts 7:7 'But I will punish the nation they serve,' said God, 'and afterwards they will leave and worship me in this place.'

2 Timothy 1:3 I constantly thank my God—whom I serve with a clear conscience, as my ancestors did—when I remember you in my prayers night and day,

Revelation 19:5 A voice came from the throne, saying, "Praise our God, all who serve and fear him, from the least important to the most important."

Chapter VI.

A Call to Action

Daniel 10:13 However, the prince of the kingdom of Persia opposed me for 21 days. Then—look!—Michael, one of the chief angels, came to assist me. I had been detained there near the kings of Persia.

Daniel 12:1 "'At that time Michael will arise, the great prince who will stand up on behalf of your people, and a time of trouble will come like there has never been since nations began until that time. Also at that time, your people will be delivered—everyone who will have been written in the book.

1 Corinthians 3: 13 the workmanship of each person will become evident, for the day of judgment will show what it is, because it will be revealed with fire, and the fire will test the quality of each person's action.

Matthew 8:10 When Jesus heard this, he was amazed and told those who were following him, "I tell you with certainty, not even in Israel have I found this kind of faith!

Matthew 8:26 He asked them, "Why are you afraid, you who have little faith?" Then he got up and rebuked the winds and the sea, and there was a great calm.

Matthew 17:20 He told them, "Because of your lack of faith. I tell you with certainty, if you have faith like a grain of mustard seed, you can say to this mountain, 'Move from here to there,' and it will move, and nothing will be impossible for you.

Matthew 21:12 Then Jesus went into the Temple, threw out everyone who was selling and buying in the Temple, and overturned the moneychangers' tables and the chairs of those who sold doves.

Matthew 21:13 He told them, "It is written, 'My house is to be called a house of prayer,' but you are turning it into a hideout for bandits!"

Matthew 21:15 But when the high priests and the scribes saw the amazing things that he had done and the children shouting in the Temple, "Hosanna to the Son of David," they became furious

Matthew 21:21 Jesus answered them, "I tell you with certainty, if you have faith and do not doubt, not only will you be able to do what has been done to the fig tree, but you will also say to this mountain, 'Be removed and thrown into the sea,' and it will happen.

Mark 4:40 He asked them, "Why are you such cowards? Don't you have any faith yet?"

Mark 10:52 Jesus told him, "Go. Your faith has made you well." At once the Man could see again, and he began to follow Jesus down the road.

Mark 11:15 When they came to Jerusalem, he went into the Temple and began to throw out those who were selling and those who were buying in the Temple. He overturned the moneychangers' tables and the chairs of those who sold doves.

Mark 11:16 He wouldn't even let anyone carry a vessel through the Temple.

Mark 11:17 Then he began to teach them: "It is written, is it not, 'My house is to be called a house of prayer for all nations'? But you have turned it into a hideout for bandits!"

Mark 11:18 When the high priests and elders heard this, they began to look for a way to kill him, because they were afraid of him, since the whole crowd was amazed at his teaching.

Mark 11:22 Jesus told his disciples, "Have faith in God!

Luke 5:20 When Jesus saw their faith, he said, "Mister, your sins are forgiven."

Luke 17:19 Then he told the Man, "Get up, and go home! Your faith has made you well."

Luke 18:42 So Jesus told him, "See again! Your faith has made you well."

Luke 19:45 Then Jesus went into the Temple and began to throw out those who were selling things.

Luke 19:46 He told them, "It is written, 'My house is to be called a house of prayer,' but you have turned it into a hideout for bandits!"

Luke 19:47 Then he began teaching in the Temple every day. The high priests, the scribes, and the leaders of the people kept looking for a way to kill him,

John 2:15 After making a whip out of cords, he drove all of them out of the Temple, including the sheep and the cattle. He scattered the coins of the moneychangers and knocked over their tables.

John 2:16 Then he told those who were selling the doves, "Take these things out of here! Stop making my Father's house a marketplace!"

Acts 11:24 For he was a good Man, full of the Holy Spirit and faith. And so a large number of people was brought to the Lord.

Acts 16:5 So the churches continued to be strengthened in the faith and to increase in numbers every day.

Acts 26:18 You will help them understand and turn them from darkness to light and from Satan's control to God, so that their sins will be forgiven and they will receive a share among those who are sanctified by faith in me.'

Romans 1:12 that is, that we may be mutually encouraged by each other's faith, both yours and mine.

2 Corinthians 10:15 We are not boasting about work done by others that cannot be evaluated. On the contrary, we cherish the hope that your faith may continue to grow and enlarge our sphere of action among you until it overflows.

2 Corinthians 13:5 Keep examining yourselves to see whether you are continuing in the faith. Test yourselves! You know, don't you, that Jesus the Messiah lives in you? Could it be that you are failing the test?

Galatians 1:23 The only thing they kept hearing was this: "The Man who used to persecute us is now proclaiming the faith he once tried to destroy!"

Galatians 6:1 Brothers, if a person is caught doing something wrong, those of you who are spiritual should restore that person gently. Watch out for yourself so that you are not tempted as well.

Galatians 6:10 So then, whenever we have the opportunity, let's practice doing good to everyone, especially to the family of faith.

Colossians 2:5 For although I am physically absent, I am with you in spirit, rejoicing to see how stable you are and how firm your faith in the Messiah is.

1 Thessalonians 1:3 In the presence of our God and Father, we constantly remember how your faith is active, your love is hard at work, and your hope in our Lord Jesus the Messiah is enduring.

1 Thessalonians 1:8 From you the word of the Lord has spread out not only in Macedonia and Achaia, but also in every place where your faith in God has become known. As a result, we do not need to say anything about it.

1 Thessalonians 3:2 and send Timothy, our brother who works with us for God in the gospel of the Messiah, to strengthen and encourage you in your faith,

1 Thessalonians 5: 14 We urge you, brothers, to admonish those who are idle, cheer up those who are discouraged, and help those who are weak. Be patient with everyone

1 Timothy 4:6 If you continue to point these things out to the brothers, you will be a good servant of the Messiah Jesus, nourished by the words of the faith and the healthy teaching that you have followed closely.

1 Timothy 6:12 Fight the good fight for the faith. Keep holding on to eternal life, to which you were called and about which you gave a good testimony in front of many witnesses.

2 Timothy 4:7 I have fought the good fight. I have completed the race. I have kept the faith.

Titus 1:1 From: Paul, a servant of God, and also an apostle of Jesus the Messiah, to bring the faith to those chosen by God, along with full knowledge of the truth that leads to godliness,

Hebrews 13:7 Remember your leaders, those who have spoken God's word to you. Think about the impact of their lives, and imitate their faith.

James 1:6 But he must ask in faith, without any doubts, for the one who has doubts is like a wave of the sea that is driven and tossed by the wind.

James 2:26 For just as the body without the spirit is dead, so faith without actions is also dead.

James 5:19 My brothers, if one of you wanders away from the truth and somebody brings him back, 20you may be sure that whoever brings a sinner back from his wrong path will save his soul from death and cover a multitude of sins.

Selected Warrior Resources

Ballistics http://en.wikipedia.org/wiki/Ballistics
BBQ http://en.wikipedia.org/wiki/Bbq
Beef Jerky http://en.wikipedia.org/wiki/Beef_jerky
Beer http://en.wikipedia.org/wiki/Beer
Browning http://www.browning.com
Children http://en.wikipedia.org/wiki/Children
Cigars http://en.wikipedia.org/wiki/Cigar
Combat Use of the Double-Edged Knife, Rex Applegate
http://www.aryanalibris.com/index.php?post/Applegate-Rex-Combat-use-of-the-double-edged-fighting-knife
Compasses http://en.wikipedia.org/wiki/Compass
Ferrari
http://www.ferrari.com/Pages/Gateway.aspx?CountryId=88&CountryTitle=United+States
Fishing http://en.wikipedia.org/wiki/Fishing
Gold Bond http://www.goldbond.com
Handloading http://en.wikipedia.org/wiki/Handloading
Holsters http://en.wikipedia.org/wiki/Holsters
Home Town Hotties http://www.maxim.com/girls/hometown-hotties
Hoppe's http://www.hoppes.com
Hot Sauce http://en.wikipedia.org/wiki/Hot_sauce
Hunting http://en.wikipedia.org/wiki/Hunting
Krav Maga http://www.kravmaga.com
Meat http://en.wikipedia.org/wiki/Meat
Mixed Martial Arts (MMA) http://en.wikipedia.org/wiki/Mixed_martial_arts
National Rifle Association www.nra.org
Nosler http://www.nosler.com
Old Spice http://www.oldspice.com/en-US/home-page.aspx
Relatives http://en.wikipedia.org/wiki/Relative
Remington http://www.remington.com
Sandwiches http://en.wikipedia.org/wiki/Sandwich
Smoked Oysters http://en.wikipedia.org/wiki/Smoked_oyster
Spam http://www.spam.com/#landing
Spartan™ Races http://www.spartan.com
Sports http://en.wikipedia.org/wiki/Sport
Springfield Armory http://www.springfield-armory.com
The Three Stooges http://en.wikipedia.org/wiki/The_three_stooges
Time http://en.wikipedia.org/wiki/Time
Top RaMen https://www.nissinfoods.com/products/TopRaMen
Trucks http://en.wikipedia.org/wiki/Truck
U. S. Army Civil Disturbances
http://armypubs.army.mil/doctrine/DR_pubs/dr_a/pdf/atp3_39x33.pdf
U. S. Army Combat Training with Pistols, M9 and M11
http://armypubs.army.mil/doctrine/DR_pubs/dr_a/pdf/fm3_23x35.pdf
U. S. Army Combatives http://www.usarmycombatives.com

U. S. Army Counterinsurgency Operations
http://fas.org/irp/doddir/army/fmi3-07-22.pdf
U. S. Army MarksManship Guide M16-/M4 Series Weapons
http://armypubs.army.mil/doctrine/DR_pubs/dr_a/pdf/fm3_22x9c1.pdf
U. S. Army Pocket Physical Fitness Guide
https://www.goarmy.com/content/dam/goarmy/downloaded_assets/pt_guide/pocket-pt-guide.pdf
U. S. Army Tactics in Counterinsurgency
http://armypubs.army.mil/doctrine/DR_pubs/dr_a/pdf/fm3_24x2.pdf
U. S. Marine Corps Martial Arts Program (MCMAP)
file:///C:/aaaa/Offense/MCRP%203-02B%20PT%201.pdf
U. S. Marines Survival, Evasion, and Recovery
http://www.marines.mil/Portals/59/Publications/MCRP%203-02H%20Survival,%20Evasion%20and%20Recovery.pdf
United States Practical Shooters Association (USPSA) http://www.uspsa.org
Vienna Sausages http://www.armour-star.com/prod_vienna.asp
W.C. Fields http://en.wikipedia.org/wiki/W.C._Fields
Watches http://en.wikipedia.org/wiki/Watches
Weather http://en.wikipedia.org/wiki/Weather
Whiskey http://en.wikipedia.org/wiki/Whisky
Winchester http://www.winchesterguns.com
Wine http://en.wikipedia.org/wiki/Wine
Woman http://en.wikipedia.org/wiki/Woman

A Warrior's Short Life

PFC DONALD J. SLATTERY, 32377286
Third Infantry Division
15th Infantry Regiment
F Company Medical Detachment
KIA: 1 March 1944

My Uncle Donald J. Slattery graduated from St. John's High School in Plattsburgh, New York, in 1940. He attended Plattsburgh Business Institute, passed his Civil Service examination, and then received an appointment to the Binghamton State Hospital in Binghamton, New York. He was drafted into the U.S. Army on June 10, 1942 and was sent overseas October 18, 1942.[1]

High School
Graduation 1940

Donald was an enthusiastic draftee but he wasn't unique because many others of his generation were the same. However, the mother of one of Donald's close friends bought a herd of cattle so her son would not be drafted. At the time milk production was considered an essential war industry making the Men involved exempt from the draft.

In the early- and mid-stages of World War II Winston Churchill doggedly lobbied the Allies to follow his strategic vision of attacking Germany through the "Soft Underbelly" of Europe. Churchill thought his strategy would be more effective than the Allies' cross-channel assault on "Fortress Europe" named "Operation Overlord".

Donald's destiny was made at the Allied Casablanca Conference in January 1943. Churchill states in his book Closing the Ring:

> Casablanca Conference in January decided to invade Sicily after the capture of Tunis. This great enterprise, known by the code name "Husky", presented new and formidable problems.[2]

General Eisenhower considered that Sicily should only be attacked if our purpose was to clear the Mediterranean sea-route. If our real purpose was to invade and defeat Italy he thought that our proper initial objectives were Sardinia and Corsica, "since these islands lie on the flank of the long Italian boot and would force a very much greater dispersion of enemy

117

strength in Italy than the mere occupation of Sicily, which lies off the mountainous toe of the peninsula." This was no doubt a military opinion of a high authority, though one I could not share. But political forces play their part, and the capture of Sicily and the direct invasion of Italy were to bring about results of a far more swift and far-reaching character.[3]

Donald received training as an Army Medic and was assigned to the Third Infantry Division, 15th Infantry Regiment Medical Detachment, Company F. First, he served in North Africa then was part of the invading force of Sicily. On August 6, 1943, he received a Silver Star for his heroic actions during combat operations in San Fratello, Sicily in support of Operation "Husky", the Allied code name for the capture of Sicily. The following is an extract from his citation:

Italy, 1943
Donald J. Slattery is
on the far right.

HEADQUARTERS THIRD INFANTRY DIVISION
A.P.O. 3
6 September 1943
GENRAL ORDERS)
             :
No.   62)

AWARD OF THE SILVER STAR

XXXX   E-X-T-R-A-C-T   XXXX

DONALD J. SLATTERY, 32377286, Private First Class, Medical Detachment, 15th Infantry Regiment. For gallantry in action. During the attack against enemy positions near San Fratello, Sicily, 6 August 1943, Pfc SLATTERY, an aid man with Company "F", repeatedly went out into intense enemy mortar and machine gun fire to administer first aid to the wounded. In order to reach the wounded of an adjacent company not his own, he several times crossed 200-600 yards of open terrain, covered with anti-personal mines, and swept by fire from four enemy machine guns and 40 rifleman, and intense mortar fire. During these trips men were wounded on either side of him, one man being seriously wounded by machine gun fire 10 yards distant, another receiving a shrapnel wound while but 5 yards from Pfc SLATTERY, who continued in his untiring efforts to bring first aid to the wounded. Pfc SLATTERY'S bravery under heavy enemy fires, his gallant devotion to duty, resulting in the saving of many lives of members of his own and adjacent companies, reflect the finest traditions of the Medical Corps and upon himself and the entire military service.

XXXX   E-X-T-R-A-C-T   XXXX

By command of Major General TRUSCOTT:

On March 1, 1944 Donald's unit was heavily engaged in battle on the Anzio beachhead to fulfill Churchill's strategy of attacking the "soft underbelly" of Europe. Although Churchill did not agree with Operation "Husky" strategy he graciously memorialized the struggle by sending the following telegram to President Roosevelt:

> I must send you my warmest congratulations on the great fighting of your troops, particularly the United States 3rd Infantry Division, in the Anzio beach-head. I am always deeply moved to think of our men fighting side by side in so many fierce battles and of the inspiring additions to our history which these famous episodes will make. Of course I have been very anxious about the beach-head, where we have so little ground to give. The stakes are very high on both sides now, and the suspense is long-drawn. I feel sure we shall win both here and at Cassiono.[4]

During the battle of Anzio Donald ran out on the battlefield numerous times to provide life-saving medical treatment and to evacuate the wounded. On his last mission he reached two wounded soldiers and was preparing to evacuate them when an artillery shell landed close by killing him and the two soldiers.

Donald J. Slattery's closed casket funeral in the living room of my Grandparents' house. I have his Silver Star and Purple Heart

The blast was so intense that his body was not in any condition to be viewed necessitating a closed-casket funeral. He was only 24 years old.

An interesting and unanswered question about Donald's death is why his body was shipped back to his hometown to be buried. Because of the many logistical problems thousands of America's war dead was buried overseas never returning home to their loved ones.

The death of my uncle devastated my grandparents, my aunt (his twin), and my father. My Grandmother was especially grieved because she knew that Donald had volunteered, whereas his friend stayed home in relative safety to milk cows.

On January 27, 1948 my Grandmother Laurena Slattery founded Clinton County, New York, Chapter 30 of the American Gold Star Mothers. On February 7, 1948 she was appointed President.[5] She was instrumental in raising funds to build the Gold Star Mothers Monument in Trinity Park, Plattsburgh, New York, which was dedicated in December 1950 "to honor the war dead and our freedom and what that stands for."[6]

My Grandfather was very politically influential and ran unsuccessfully as a Democrat for the

Presentation of the flag to my Grandmother at the cemetery. My Grandfather is on my Grandmother's right. My father (age 16) is standing on my Grandmother's left.

Clinton County seat in the New York State Assembly in 1942.[7] He was the Plumbing Inspector for the City of Plattsburgh, a very prestigious position at the time, and he was active in city and county politics.

My father enlisted in the U. S. Air Force and was promoted to Staff Sergeant well ahead of his peers serving with him in a medical unit in Korea. He was honorably discharged and he returned home to marry my mother and raise a boisterous family of six children.

The death of my uncle as a direct consequence of Churchill's "Soft Underbelly" strategy has resonated through my life as well as that of my siblings and their children.

Inspired by my uncle's short life I joined the Army ROTC program at the State University of New York at Cortland. Following graduate school at Long Island University I was commissioned a Second Lieutenant in the U. S. Army Medical Services Corps and served almost 10 years. Due to injuries and other considerations, I left the

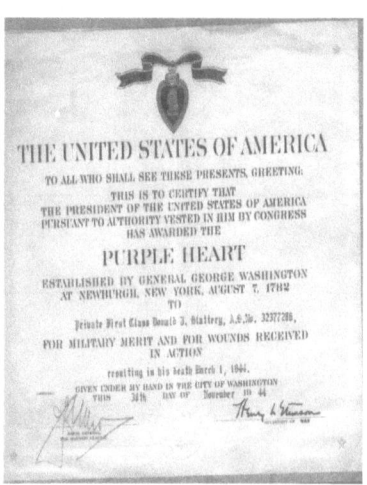

Donald J. Slattery awarded a Purple Heart for "…wounds received in action resulting in his death March 1, 1944".

Army and worked in the medical field. Each of my four sisters works in the medical field. My sister Connie is a Registered Nurse as was our Grandmother.

If my uncle had lived he could have had a long and full life with a family of his own and I, and many others, would have been greatly enriched by his life.

Notes

Gold Star Mothers
Monument
Trinity Park, Plattsburgh,
New York

1. <u>Plattsburgh Press Republican</u>, 170 Margaret Street, Plattsburgh, New York, 12901, October 23, 1943.
2. <u>Closing The Ring</u>, Winston S. Churchill, Houghton Mifflin Company, Boston, 1979, Page 23.
3. <u>Closing the Ring</u>, Pages 23-24.
4. <u>Closing the Ring</u>, Page 434.
5. <u>Plattsburgh Press Republican</u>, June 7, 2003.
6. <u>Plattsburgh Press Republican</u>, February 3, 1973.
7. <u>The Political Graveyard</u>, A Database of Historic Cemeteries, Internet, http://politicalgraveyard.com.

Index

www.ingramcontent.com/pod-product-compliance
Lightning Source LLC
Chambersburg PA
CBHW050455290526
45786CB00006B/2305